PROFIT
WRITE

PROFIT WRITE

HOW TO CREATE BOOKS THAT GROW YOUR BUSINESS, BRAND, AND IMPACT

LANETTE POTTLE

Magenta Acorn Press

Profit Write: How to Create Books That Grow Your Business, Brand, and Impact

Copyright © 2024 by Lanette Pottle

All rights reserved. No part of this publication may be reproduced, distributed, or transmitted in any form or by any means, including photocopying, recording, or other electronic or mechanical methods, without the prior written permission of the publisher, except in the case of brief quotations embodied in critical reviews and certain other noncommercial uses permitted by copyright law. To request permission, email support@shegetspublished.com - include "Profit Write reprint permission" in the subject line.

Magenta Acorn Press | Robbinston, Maine

Cover & Interior Design: George Stevens, G Sharp Design, LLC
Edited by: Laurel Robinson Editorial Services
Author Photo Credit: Danielle Pease Photography

ISBN: 979-8-9913843-0-8 (paperback)
979-8-9913843-1-5 (e-book)
Library of Congress Control Number: 2024917436

Disclaimer: This publication is designed to provide accurate and authoritative information regarding the subject matter covered. It is sold with the understanding that neither the author nor the publisher is engaged in rendering legal, investment, or accounting services. While the publisher and author have used their best efforts in preparing this book, they make no representations or warranties with respect to the accuracy or completeness of the contents of this book and specifically disclaim any implied warranties of merchantability or fitness for a particular purpose. The advice and strategies contained herein may not be suitable for your situation. You should consult with a professional when appropriate. Neither the publisher nor the author shall be liable for any loss of profit or any other commercial damages, including but not limited to special, incidental, consequential, personal, or other damages.

To honor and respect the privacy of individuals, certain names and identifying characteristics have been altered.

For my clients—past, present, and future.
You are creating a tsunami of positive change in
the world. Thank you for your contributions and
willingness to do the work.

TABLE OF CONTENTS

PART I: BEFORE YOU BEGIN

Chapter 1   A Word from Your Author 3

Chapter 2   Clear the Path 11

Chapter 3   Set the Stage 21

Chapter 4   Embrace the Truth 29

PART II: GATHER WHAT YOU NEED

Chapter 5   Start With the End in Mind 39

Chapter 6   Know Your Audience 49

Chapter 7   Plan the Journey 57

Chapter 8   Commit to Connection 67

PART III: TIME TO BUILD

Chapter 9   Create Your Outline 81

Chapter 10   Hatch a Plan 93

Chapter 11   Celebrate the Mess 101

Chapter 12   Add the Sparkle and Shine 109

PART IV: PREPARE TO RISE

Chapter 13   Raise Your Visibility............................121

Chapter 14   Decide and Publish 131

Chapter 15   Rally to Launch................................143

Chapter 16   Keep Going 153

Acknowledgments 161

Research Roundup 165

Create More Profitability.....................................167

Work with Lanette..169

Learn About Future Events..................................171

About the Author...173

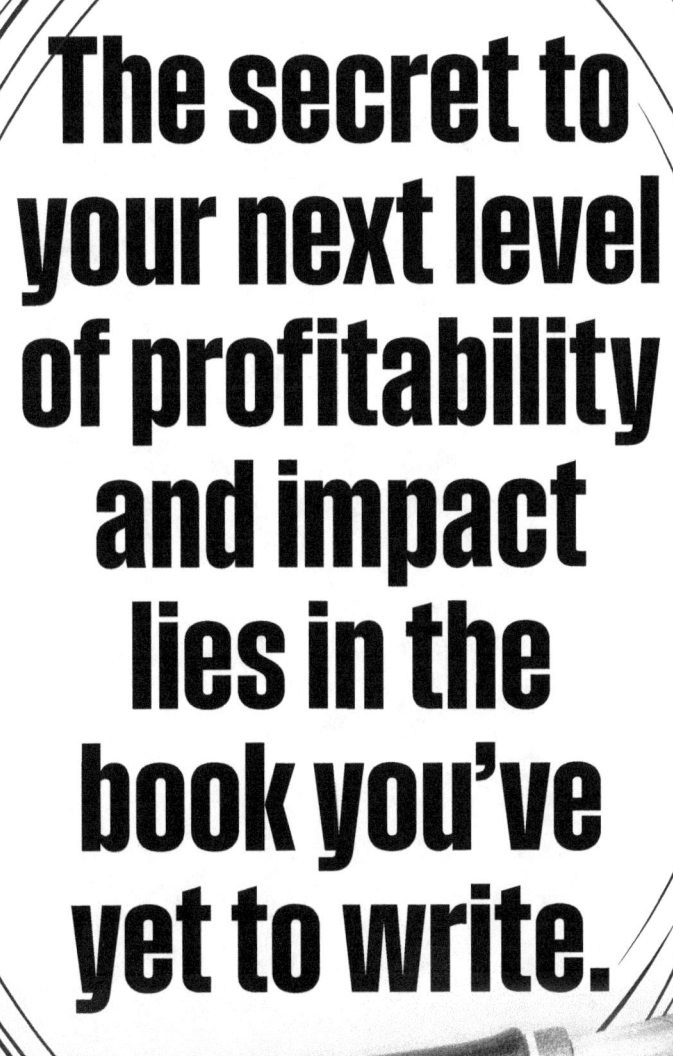

PART I

BEFORE YOU BEGIN

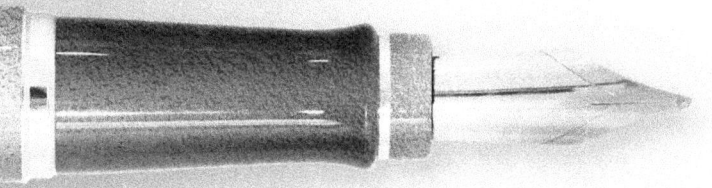

CHAPTER 1

A WORD FROM YOUR AUTHOR

Hey, hey, my soon-to-be-published author friend!

I know you probably don't consider yourself a writer, so the very first thing I want you to know is it's not a prerequisite to the work we're about to delve into together.

Cue the deep sigh of relief.

This book is *not* an academic guide for developing your technical skills or honing your writing craft. I'm not the person to write that book; it's not where my skills, talents, or brilliance lie. But connection and strategy related to books and business? That's a completely different story.

And make no mistake about it, connection and strategy are exactly what you need—in your business and with your book—to be profitable and make the impact you desire.

I don't know exactly where your personal brilliance lies, but I know beyond a shadow of a doubt you have experience, wisdom, and knowledge that can serve others.

You are a subject matter expert…in something…probably in *many* things. What might seem like second nature to you is elusive to others. Showing them how to attain it for themselves is a gift.

Think about where you were three, four, or five years ago. Wouldn't it have been a godsend to have the knowledge you have now? Of course it would have. And it will be to the people who read your book, too.

The good news (for both of us) is we don't have to be writers with Master of Fine Arts degrees to create books that spark transformation and impact our readers; we just need to share what we know in a way they can understand and receive.

Even better news?

We don't have to do that all on our own.

I'll get you started in the areas of organization and structure. Then, once you get your ideas and expertise out of your head and down on paper, you'll be ready for the support of someone whose genius is in editing…and let them do *their* magic.

A good editor puts the sparkle and shine on our thoughts, stories, systems, processes, methodologies…the works. They help polish our writing to reflect our voice in its very best version.

Fair warning: it will be messy on the way there, but when you're holding the finished product in your hands, even *you* will be impressed. I've seen it happen time and again—new authors holding the final version of their book and marveling at what they've created.

Now that you know what this book is *not*, let's chat about what it *is*: a guide serving as a needle-moving tool you'll use to stand out and elevate yourself from being a "best-kept secret" to a recognized and sought-after leader in your field—one who attracts new clients and celebration-worthy opportunities.

As a natural by-product of the visibility associated with publishing your book in the *Profit Write* way, you will stand out. It will help people further get to know, like, and trust you.

Soooooo...I've been doing this long enough to know that you may have a little doubt niggling at the back of your brain right about now...wanting to believe it but still wobbling on the fence, wondering why a book really matters so much in building your business. There are a lot of reasons, like keeping you top of mind by being in the room long before arriving and long after you leave (we'll talk about others, too), but for now, I want to tell you a story about a colleague of mine, Howard, as one very tangible example of why a book matters to your business. With more than twenty years' experience and as a recognized high-performing expert in his field, Howard was well known and trusted in his local market area. He'd even broken onto the scene of some very high-ranking podcasts, landed (unpaid) gigs at big national events as a breakout speaker, and hosted his own sold-out conferences.

But when he went to one national-level event organizer whom he'd grown to know well (after being part of their large event for multiple years) and asked what he had to do to "graduate" from breakout speaker to speaking on the main stage, he was flat-out told they didn't slate anyone to speak for opening or closing keynote who didn't have a book on the topic they'd be speaking about.

The truth is, Howard was a more knowledgeable and compelling speaker in his topic area than some of those who had graced the main stage, but because he hadn't yet written a book, none of his talent, wisdom, or experience mattered.

Is this fair? One could make an argument that it's not, but the reality is, *fairness doesn't really matter here.*

I'm sure you haven't gotten this far in life and business to be under the illusion that "fair" is the criterion for all decisions made.

Armed with this new information, Howard had a choice to make: write the book he was capable of writing but kept putting off as a "someday" project and shoot for the prestigious stage, or keep doing what he was doing and accept the fact that he wouldn't speak on that "benchmark" stage he'd set his sights on.

Howard chose to write the book.

He hired an experienced book coach to guide him through the structural process and provide accountability throughout the writing phase. Then he turned his manuscript over to a hybrid publisher to go through editing, design, and publication. In less than a year his book was available. It was good...not just something he slapped together but something he could really be proud to have his name on.

The following year Howard was a paid keynote speaker on that big stage—arguably one of the most important in his industry. And from there he gained new clients, new speaking opportunities, an overall uplevel in his professional life.

Howard learned the truth about how books make you stand out and create profitability in your business. He gained an understanding and appreciation of how books are to business what compounding interest is to wealth: a critical component of growth—and a gift that keeps on giving.

For most people, the payoff of a book doesn't come in the form of royalties; it comes in the form of new and greater opportunities. Books spark what I call the *Credibility Continuum*—an ongoing cycle of visibility that leads to a boost in authority and expansion of your network, which leads to new opportunities, including PR/media.

One stat reported during the segment I was invited to do for the nationally syndicated television show *The List* in early 2023 highlighted this. Before introducing me for the piece ("Boost Your Credibility with a Book"), co-host Jimmy Rhoades reported that "being the author of a book can increase your professional credibility by up to 300 percent." Yowzer! See what I mean? The level of potential your book holds for your business and brand is no joke.

So, if all of this is the case (spoiler alert: it is!), then what's standing in the way of getting started?

The simple surface answers I typically get are things like, "I don't have enough time...or money...or resources." But when we dig deeper, the truth is more likely to be rooted in the fear of judgment.

Writing a book can be accurately described as an exercise in personal growth. The process can awaken old fears or false beliefs we hold about ourselves—ones that we don't talk about openly yet, the ones that hold us back. The biggest ways I see this present itself are through things like perfectionist tendencies and impostor syndrome, which can lead to self-sabotage.

That's why we'll tackle the mindset needed to get you ready for what's to come, before digging into the content that will help you...

- choose the book idea that best supports your current goals,
- build your author platform to gain visibility,
- adopt your overall book strategy,
- create your writing plan...and help you stick to it.

We'll also touch on publishing and launch options, because let's face it, it's the question everyone asks when they decide to write a book: "How will this even get published, and how will people know about it?"

We're going to take a closer look at all this in the pages ahead. Parts 1 and 2 of the book will prepare you with all you need for the process; parts 3 and 4 will equip you to create and execute on your plan. In each chapter I've provided Profit Write Ponderings for you—questions to get you thinking about how the material you read applies to you and your book project.

For now, I want to reassure you that you're in the right place at the right time and to encourage you to experience what's to come with an open mind. It might feel uncomfortable, but it's time to stand out in a bigger way. This isn't just about people knowing your name; it's for a much greater purpose.

> **When good people (like you) make great money, they create incredible impact in their communities and the world at-large.**

Lean into *that* and let's go!

In your corner,
Lanette

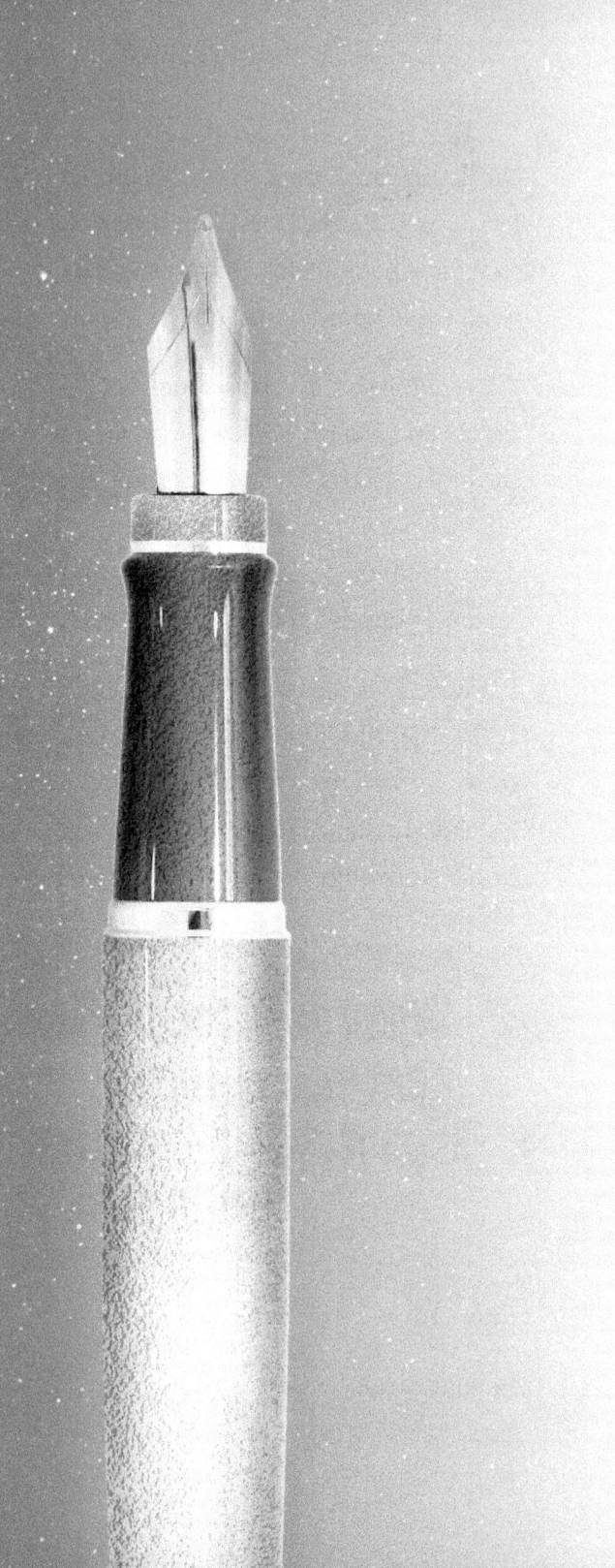

CHAPTER 2

CLEAR THE PATH

Creating a clear path for book creation starts by cleaning up the self-made obstacles that live as thoughts in our minds:

- Impostor syndrome
- Perfectionism
- Negative self-talk
- Doubts

This is the recurring garbage we all wrestle with from time to time, so let's get ahead of it as you prepare to create your book. But first a disclaimer…

I recognize this may be an area where you support your clients or team, but my role in this moment is to shine a light on *your* blind spots. As one business owner to another, I think we can agree—it's generally easier to coach others than it is ourselves, because our perspective gets skewed when the challenges are up close and personal...not to mention the fact that coaching ourselves means *we* then have to do the work.

Now that we have that out of the way, let's reframe these feelings, shall we?

During a conversation I was having at a networking event with a sharp, accomplished woman, she candidly shared that she had thought about writing a book. "But," she went on to say, "I can't help but think, *Why would they pick up my book if it were sitting side by side on a book seller's shelf next to one of Mel Robbins's?*"

"Why wouldn't they pick up both?" I asked with curiosity.

Before she said anything, a visible shift occurred in her body language. You could almost see a light bulb go on. Our bookshelves are filled with books written by a variety of authors sharing their unique perspectives on the same or similar topics.

Maybe it isn't Mel Robbins, but is there someone you've built up in your mind as the author you compare yourself against?

When those comparison-based thoughts show up, remind yourself that there's room for your book and your unique perspective. It's not an "either/or" decision—it's an "and."

Sometimes a simple reframing like that shifts our perspective and gets us back on track. Other times it takes a deeper dive.

This three-step approach can help you move through those tougher moments.

Step One: Identify

Being able to name what you are experiencing allows you to recognize it for what it is—a feeling, *not fact*. Catch yourself in the act and make a physical response—maybe it's making a statement out loud or snapping a band on your wrist.

Step Two: Interrogate

It's time to ask questions and get to the bottom of the situation. It might be as simple as taking a deep breath and asking yourself, *What's really going on here?* or *What's bringing this up again?*

But if it's a particularly stubborn occurrence of impostor syndrome, I love the questions author Byron Katie refers to as The Work to better identify the falsehood of my feelings and beliefs.

Walk yourself through this series of questions:

> **Is this true?**
> *(Is it true I am a fraud?)*
>
> **Can you be absolutely sure it's true?**
> *(How can I be absolutely sure I'm a fraud?)*

How do you react when you believe that thought?
(How does it make me feel when I believe I'm a fraud?)

Who would you be without that thought?
(Who would I be if I didn't feel like a fraud?)

Step Three: Neutralize

Depending on how deep you went on step two, you may have already achieved this, but in case you didn't, you can begin to take the power away from the negative, fraudulent feelings by revisiting all the evidence you've created of your competence.

One of the most frequently quoted lines from my TEDx Talk applies here too:

> **You may be a beginner at this thing you are getting ready to do, but you are not a beginner at life.**

Many of the skill sets you've developed in other areas of your life are transferable and will support you in your writing endeavors. Place your focus here.

Hint: Take preemptive action and create a success file—something that can be easily accessed in times of doubt. You'll want to include accomplishments, accolades, words of thanks and praise—basically anything that reinforces and reminds you of what you are capable of and the impact your efforts have had on others.

Another tool you might find helpful here is the use of affirmations or mantras—positive statements that resonate with you...ones that you can repeat to disrupt the negative self-talk running on a continuous loop.

Here are a few favorites:

> *Impostor syndrome likes to sneak in when I'm stepping into uncharted territory. When it shows up, it only confirms I am on my growth edge.*
>
> *I am committed to focusing on my strengths and talents, reminding myself that I am more than capable of accomplishing my book goals.*
>
> *I am constantly evolving and improving, understanding that my journey of self-discovery and growth is what makes me a capable and authentic author—and leader.*
>
> *(Like these? I have a whole booklet full of writing affirmations you can download for free. Use the QR code in the Resource Roundup section at the back of the book to access them.)*

Another kind of doubt or false belief that might be showing up right about now might sound like this:

> *I don't know enough about how to get a book published, and until I learn all that, there's no sense in even tackling the writing part.*

True confession: I had the same thoughts myself. GASP! It's a big reason it took seven years and fifty-six days for me to publish my first book.

It also makes me think of the first conversation I ever had with a bestselling author. I had been following her journey online for years, so having the opportunity to connect was a real treat.

"What's the most important question I can answer for you today?" were her generous first words to me.

I had a million questions, but what tumbled out of my mouth was, "Oh gosh! I have so many, but the biggest one is what did you have to do to become a bestselling author?"

As naive (and cringe-y) as that question was, she graciously used it as an opportunity to give me a tremendous gift.

Instead of getting into the weeds with me about strategy and tactics that would have been like a foreign language to me at the time—and could never be covered in a fifteen-minute call—she asked me a simple but profound question:

"Do you have a completed manuscript?"

Gulp. "Not yet," I shared with embarrassment.

"Why don't we spend our time focused on how to get that done? Because without it you will never have the opportunity to become a bestselling author."

This gift of learning the better question to ask is one I frequently share with others, and now share with you. Consider it as you continue reading this book and choosing where you'll place your focus and action.

I've given you lots to think about, but before we move out of this section and into how to create an environment for your writing, there's another resource I want to share: *The 5 Author Freakouts*, the bestselling book by Thanet House Books CEO Julie Anne Eason.

Julie has worked with a wide variety of clients, including well-known online entrepreneurs such as Alex Hormozi and Russell Brunson, and says that *all* authors experience some, if not all, of the five freakouts during the course of writing and publishing their books. (Translation: You're in good company!) The book is fun, useful, and relatable; it's worth checking out.

CHAPTER HIGHLIGHTS

- Identify feelings behind perceived obstacles and challenges of writing your book.
- Interrogate your thoughts.
- Neutralize disempowering beliefs.
- Gather evidence of your strengths and success.
- Use affirmations to bolster your belief.
- Ask better questions of yourself and others.

PROFIT WRITE PONDERINGS

1. What thoughts and beliefs are getting in the way of writing your book?

2. What reframes will you put into play to support yourself in clearing the path to writing success?

3. How will you stay anchored in empowering thoughts and beliefs?

4. Where can you ask better questions of yourself and others as you move through your book creation journey?

5. Which resources will you add to your toolbox?

CHAPTER 3

SET THE STAGE

Location

Would you be surprised to learn that *where* we choose to write matters? Not only from the perspective of the physical location but how we *feel* in that space and how our brain reacts to it.

The right space for you might not be in your home or office—or at least that may be the case on occasion. If you live in an area with a coffee shop or coworking space nearby that has great energy, that might be a great alternative. Sometimes it might be a spot in nature. Far less common is the romanticized escape to the mountain lodge or lakeside cabin where you isolate until your full manuscript is written.

Even with a writing plan (which we'll talk about later) and good space, sometimes when we sit down to write, we're just not feeling it. This is often mislabeled as writer's block, but

I think of it more like trying to slam our mind into high gear from a cold start.

Rituals

There are quick and simple ways to help signal to your brain that it's time to engage in the writing process: rituals. These are not a one-size-fits-all solution. In fact, what works today might not fit tomorrow. That's why I encourage people to build a collection of choices to pull from—some do this from a literal sense, others do it figuratively.

If you want to land on the literal side of this, what you can do is set aside ten to fifteen minutes specifically to think of a variety of prewriting rituals. Record each one on a slip of paper, then fold them and place them in a jar. Each day your ritual then becomes pulling an idea from your ritual jar and doing that thing. Very meta, I know, but for some people it works like a charm because it keeps things interesting. Plus, a funny phenomenon happens: if you choose a piece of paper that lists a ritual you're not into that day, your subconscious mind will automatically reveal what you were really hoping you'd pick. Do that instead.

Clever, right? But the truth is you get to set the tone for everything. If you want it to feel playful, that's one way you can go about it. I suspect you can think of others.

As I'm writing this book, one of the rituals that has consistently served me well is using some of my favorite essential oils (a combination of clementine and peppermint) in a beautiful diffuser that emits a soft light. I typically write in my office...but I also do a whole lot of other kinds of creating there. So when I'm ready to work on the book, I set up the diffuser, take in a few deep breaths of the aroma, then click on the study music channel on Pandora and settle in at my desk to write. Just before I do, I pull out my InterGalactic Thinking Putty (yes, it's really a thing...think fun, sparkly younger cousin of Silly Putty) and stretch it for a minute or two. It's like this combination magically activates the part of my brain that knows it's time to sit down and have a conversation with you.

You'll find what works best to prime your mind for writing, but to give you a head start on building your bag of tricks, here are a few rituals that have worked for me, clients, and other writer friends I've polled:

- Light a candle—one that has a particular scent or specific sound (think WoodWick Crackle candles) or meaning.
- Sit in a cozy spot or space.
- Slip into a soft, fuzzy sweater (kinda like Mister Rogers at the start of each episode).

- Listen to classical music or binaural beats.
- Sip tea or coffee from a special mug.
- Pray or meditate, asking your higher power to allow the right words to flow through you.
- Hold a pen that feels good in your hand (even if you're going to use your computer when it's time to write).
- Pull an oracle or affirmation card.
- Do a timed free write to do a brain dump of everything on your mind other than your book.
- Go for a long walk to let ideas percolate and surface, then go home and start writing.
- Doodle or scribble to activate the creative mind.
- Start the night before. Go to bed purposely thinking about writing.

Time

Before we move on, I also want to point out that the time at which you write is as important as physical location and developing writing rituals.

One thing shared like gospel is that writing first thing in the morning is the time *serious* writers write. Rituals are built around this as if it's fact, but that's simply not true for everyone.

I'm raising my hand high here as one of them. Occasionally, I wake up inspired to write from the moment my feet hit the floor, but that's rarely the case. I need to ease into the day; then maybe an hour or so later, I hit my zone for writing capacity. More consistently, though, it's the evening hours when my creativity kicks into overdrive. It's not always convenient, but trying to fight it is simply not productive for me.

Instead of feeling pressure to conform to what you hear is the best time for writing or what works exquisitely for others, pay attention to when you feel most in your creative flow. What's that sweet spot in your day when your energy level is good? If you can't quickly name it, try doing a personal energy audit. Consciously make note of your energy levels throughout the day. Graph them on a chart and notice trends. Often as busy business owners we can tend to think every day is different—that patterns don't exist because we don't have a routine schedule—when overall, our peak energy times don't vary all that much.

Once you've identified the patterns in your energy and creativity flow, experiment with adding writing sprints—short, focused periods of time—to your schedule.

If your schedule is severely restricted and the only window of opportunity to write *is* first thing in the morning whether you like it or not, my friend Tabitha's ritual might work for you. It's what she does in the evening before bed that sets her up for a successful writing session in the morning. She has a space tidied up and ready to go, but she also tidies her mind, feeding her subconscious a thought about what she is going to write the next day so that it's percolating under the surface as she sleeps. When she wakes up, 99 percent of the time she's ready to write.

As you review this chapter, you may be able to put a big old red X through some—or many—of the ideas, but ideally, it'll spark your imagination of what may work better. Like the ritual jar, sometimes the way to get to what we like or what works is by way of figuring out what we don't like or what doesn't work.

CHAPTER HIGHLIGHTS

- Your physical environment impacts your writing flow.
- Switching up your surroundings shifts your energy and creativity.
- Writing rituals prepare your mind for writing.
- There is no single best time to write.
- Understanding your natural energy peaks and valleys allows you to better tap into your creativity zones.

PROFIT WRITE PONDERINGS

1. Where are the spaces you feel most focused and creative?

2. What time of day do you feel writing comes easiest for you?

3. What are you currently doing that helps your writing flow?

4. Would a personal energy audit be helpful for you?

5. Which ideas in this chapter are you willing to try on for size?

CHAPTER 4

EMBRACE THE TRUTH

What I'm about to share is often met with resistance, but it's something that can't be understated:

Being profitable, growing our authority, attracting clients, and elevating our influence to make the impact we desire is about *more* than writing and publishing a book...It's what we *do* with that book. We have to become visible—from the moment we decide to become an author (or at least as soon as we're aware of its importance). That's what puts all the benefits of our book into motion.

Marketing and promotion begin on day one. It's about pulling back the curtain and giving people an inside look at the process—the highs and lows of writing and publishing a book.

But nobody is going to be interested in hearing about this stuff!, you may be thinking. (No, I'm not a mind reader. But that thought has been shared with me enough that I can make a pretty educated guess.)

Let me jump in right here and tell you that's not true. We need to call this thought what it is—a belief, *not a fact.*

> **Just because doing something is uncomfortable for you doesn't mean others aren't interested.**

People are wildly curious about what it takes to get a book to market. Studies show that over 80 percent of Americans dream of writing a book, so giving them glimpses into what we're doing and how we're feeling lets them live vicariously through us.

Because of this, they'll cheer us on and want to help us succeed. We'll develop champions for our book long before it's released, and the anticipation will have people lined up to buy. Many of them will be the people who help us with our bestseller launch.

We're going to talk about this topic more than once throughout the book, because skipping the whole visibility piece will yield similar results to the cake I made one time when I forgot to add eggs—your efforts will fall flat. (And let me tell ya... it ain't pretty!)

So do I have your permission to be really blunt here?

> **If you aren't willing to talk about your book, you shouldn't write one.**

I know, it might sting a little to hear that megadose of tough love. But the saddest thing I see is brilliant people who pour their time, energy, heart, and soul into creating a book, then quietly release it into the abyss, hoping the algorithm gods will work their wonders...morphing their books onto the bestselling scene as they go about life as if they never created the thing.

Take my word for it: it's heartbreakingly awful.

That's why I'm so glad you're holding *this* book in your hands...because that's the last thing I want for you.

Yes, a book—when strategically executed—will help you grow your profits, influence, and impact—but it's not a magic trick... though it undoubtedly may *feel* like magic from time to time.

Brian Miller, a magician turned internationally acclaimed speaker and TEDx phenom, says, "Magic isn't about tricking people; it's about connection." That's the kind of magic we're going for—*connection*.

We'll look at ways to make the process simple and effective, but it will still require a conscious effort on your part to follow through. It doesn't have to take a lot of time, but it most definitely takes powerful intention.

Dedicating time before we ever write the first word of our book to reflect on why it's important to us—then recording it in a journal or someplace where we can easily access it in the future—is crucial.

Anchoring into this meaning serves as motivation when we bump up against a challenge or hiccup or discomfort in our writing or publishing plan.

Having a written record allows us to go back and remind ourselves of what we were thinking when we started the project and why it was important in the first place. That reason becomes the undercurrent of motivation.

Above all, it's the way you're *thinking* about promoting your book. Getting your mindset right around this early on makes all the difference.

If even a tiny piece of you is equating talking about your book with being a pushy salesman using icky tactics to make a sale, the time to work through this is *now*.

When you talk about your book, it's essential to remember you are providing people an opportunity. You're making them aware of how its contents may be able to help them. Profitability is certainly one of the outcomes you are looking for, but never lose sight of the fact that it is through service—how your book will serve your ideal readers/future customers, the value you provide—that'll get you there. You aren't *pushing* anything. You are simply creating awareness around something so those who need what you have can find you.

That's it. Nothing more; nothing less.

In fact, talking about your book and how it can help others is one of the most generous things you can do. When your intention is to be a "go-giver"—as Bob Burg and John David Mann describe it in their book by the same name—that's exactly how you set your message up to be received.

Embrace that truth and you'll be a whole lot closer to your goals.

CHAPTER HIGHLIGHTS

- Be willing to talk about your book early and often.
- When your intentions are rooted in service, that's how they will be received.
- Sharing is generous, not selfish.
- Invest time in resetting your mindset if the ideas in this chapter are challenging for you.

PROFIT WRITE PONDERINGS

1. What stories do you tell yourself about what it means to promote your book?

2. What's at the heart of any discomfort you feel when you think about sharing it?

3. What's your "why" anchor?

4. What steps are you willing to take to ensure you do not quietly bring your book to market?

PART II

GATHER WHAT YOU NEED

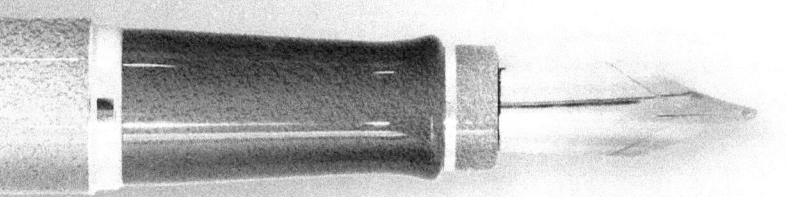

CHAPTER 5

START WITH THE END IN MIND

Just like that home remodeling project or delicious recipe you want to try for tonight's dinner, when you're writing your book, you need to be clear on what you need to have on hand to bring the mission to completion.

The first thing you need to do to accomplish this is get clear on *what* you're creating. In other words, answer the question, What's the right book, *right now*?

Sometimes to find that answer you must let go of attachments. I experienced this with a book I had 90 percent complete—*You Are a Success Magnet*.

I planned to launch this book in 2020, but with the pandemic and changes in my business, things got complicated. I had invested a lot of time, energy, and resources in getting the book to the point where it was. I didn't do it quietly either. I'd shared pictures of myself at a writing retreat, talked about various elements of the book's premise and my process on my social channels, and even gone so far as to share the many iterations of the title and cover design.

I strongly believed in the core premise of the book (that like magnets, we have the capability to attract and repel—to draw in success or push it away), and it was laid out in such a way that it would open the door to a lot of opportunity around my professional focus *at the time*—life and business strategy.

Even though I was committed to the ideas presented in that book and knew the content would be valuable to those who read it, it no longer made sense when I thought about the strategic role it could play in my business—all the reasons I first started writing it.

The year 2020 was the time when my focus began to pivot away from the type of coaching I'd been doing. And while that book is filled with relevant practices and truths I've brought over into my work with She Gets Published, the problems and focus of my ideal reader shifted. Elements of the narrative may have connected, but it was no longer solving the top-of-mind problem my future clients were wrestling with.

From that perspective, that book wasn't as directly aligned with my work today as *this* book is—even though a couple of tidbits from that book migrated here.

I could have continued to sink time and money into getting that book to market, but then what? I'd have nothing further to offer the people reading it, no place to lead them. My offerings and community are no longer in that realm. I already had books like that on the market—ones that checked the box for impact but not for elevating the new direction of my business and brand.

Even if I chose to pursue publishing that book strictly as a passion project, the time and resources it would take to design, release, and promote it would take away from what I could invest in the way I serve today.

My experience with *You Are a Success Magnet* is an example of sunk costs. Throwing more of my precious resources into that book simply because I'd already invested so much would have been shortsighted. I chose to see the value the process of writing and researching it held for me, but in the end, I made the smartest business decision for myself and moved on.

If you've had an idea for a long time, you may find yourself at a similar crossroads: do you choose to continue or begin again?

It's also very possible that you haven't gotten as far with the ideas you've been tossing around as I was with *You Are a Success Magnet*.

Maybe if we were to sit down to chat over coffee about your book idea, you'd have not just one but several brewing—all of them good. That's the blessing and the curse of wisdom, experience, and knowledge intersecting with creativity.

For someone like you who plans to use their book to open the door to new and bigger opportunities, strategy becomes the deciding factor when it comes to which idea cuts to the front of the line...and it's not always obvious at first glance. My client Charlene experienced this.

When she arrived at our two-day author jump-start intensive, she had four ideas for the book she wanted to write. A couple of them would have been easy to "phone in." She already had a lot of existing content that she could repurpose into a book. That would have checked the box of becoming an author, but when we vetted the ideas through the filter of strategy, most of them didn't pass the test.

And to be clear, it's not that these were bad ideas or that repurposing existing content is inherently a bad idea (on the contrary, sometimes it's a great idea, especially when it comes to other areas of your business, like blogs and social media); this just didn't happen to be one of them.

When we fleshed out her most desired outcome for her book, it was to lead readers to a yet-to-be-developed service offering and create a new revenue stream.

Using that lens, we went back to the menu of ideas. One stood out to hold the most potential, and wouldn't you know, it was last on her list—the one that stretched her most when she thought about developing it.

Despite the initial discomfort, the wisdom in this choice further revealed itself as we started to create the outline for her book. She could now clearly see the bones of the new program in the making. The book and the course differ in content, but the high-level topics and the flow of the material are the same.

She was able to apply strategy to the decision-making process, not only because she was clear about her goals but because she was crystal clear on who she was doing this all for. She knew her reader—what they wanted, needed, and the journey she could facilitate to get them there.

I don't want to mislead you here. This wasn't a snap-of-the-fingers quick or an inherently obvious decision. We spent a couple of hours talking through each idea, considering the pros and cons and how it strategically fit as a needle mover toward her goal.

Short of you and I getting in a room and doing the deep-dive work like Charlene and I did, the next best way to start on your decision-making process is by putting your ideas through this five-question filter:

> **1. What is my *primary* purpose for writing this book?**
> *Your answer here will not only help you select your idea but guide your strategy for getting there.*

2. Of all the ideas I'm considering, which one *most* aligns with this goal?

This question is getting you to the unbiased truth. For instance, if you find that your answer to question one is less to do with business building and more about simply fulfilling a long-held dream to write a book, it will clearly impact your answer.

3. For which of these ideas have I previously created content?

If you've created content about this topic in the past, not only is it likely an area you are more intimately familiar with, but your confidence level about writing an entire book around the idea is likely going to be higher. That in and of itself creates a higher probability you'll reduce or minimize the amount of mindset work you'll need to tap into to get your first book across the finish line. This isn't a non-negotiable, but it is about the path of least resistance.

4. Of the ideas that remain, which one(s) can I see myself still talking most passionately about in three years?

This is a biggie! But why three years? This is really a litmus test for how profitable the book will be for you, because to create momentum and get traction, you'll need to be talking about it long after you've written and published it. Your book is not the ending; it's the beginning. It creates an opening—

an opportunity—to spotlight your wisdom, experience, and thought leadership on this topic.

If, after weeding out the ideas that aren't the best to help you meet your goals, you still have more than one viable choice, then as a tie-breaking question, ask yourself this:

5. Which idea most excites me?

Leaving this question until the end is sometimes controversial. Won't everything we create be better if we're excited about it? Yes, undoubtedly. But there are a couple of things to keep in mind. If you start simply from a place of what excites you, you could very well produce a book, but it might not serve you in any meaningful way as it relates to your business. I would argue that if your goal is related to growing your business and the book idea doesn't inherently excite you on some level, any product or service offer your book leads to won't succeed in the long run.

Long-game thinking always brings the greatest rewards.

CHAPTER HIGHLIGHTS

- Be clear on your goals and motivations before selecting your book idea.

- Not all good book ideas are the right ones to help you reach your goals.

- The best book idea is not always the easiest or most comfortable.

- Sometimes walking away with sunk costs is the best decision for your book and business.

PROFIT WRITE PONDERINGS

1. What's the driving reason for you to create a book right now?

2. Do you have an old/previous book idea that it's time to retire?

3. Which book idea remains when you go through the five-question filter?

CHAPTER 6

KNOW YOUR AUDIENCE

Whether it's an in-person conversation or one that takes place through the pages of a book, it's important for us to know our audience. It's what helps us know the right information to share and how to do it in a way that it can be best received. But in our case as authors and business owners, there is something more.

Even before we begin plotting the book, we need to think about who we're writing the book for. Your book, and mine too, will surely be able to help many people, but when it comes to marketing said book, we've got to narrow our focus.

This is one place in marketing where less is more.

Let's look at an example, shall we?

Say you are a parenting coach, and you begin writing a book with the idea your intended readers are parents—moms and dads of all ages and circumstances.

While there will likely be nuggets of information inside your book that would serve all types of parents, what you say to let different groups know the book is for them, and how you talk to them inside the book, would be vastly different.

Think about it. You'd be sharing different stories, techniques, and marketing strategies for each of these groups of parents. The list below is just a sampling. (Of course, there are many more niches in the parenting space.)

- Entrepreneurial moms of toddlers
- Foster parents
- First-time dads
- Parents who are about to be empty nesters
- Parents of tweens and teens
- Work-from-home moms who are homeschooling
- Parent of differently abled children
- First-time adoptive parents
- Grandparents who have taken on parenting responsibilities
- Step-parents challenged with blending families
- Same-sex parents

As you can see, there are a lot of angles here that cover different groups under the umbrella of "parents." Each group has different problems they are trying to solve; their Google or Amazon searches will reflect this. There isn't a generic one-size-fits-all, but if you home in on the group(s) of people you want to serve beyond your book, you're off to a great start.

You've also seen this on the pages of this book—in fact, before reading nothing more than the title. It's easy to know I'm speaking specifically to people like you—interested in growing their business, brand, and impact. For my examples, I'm using clients from my own business experiences as well as other business owners I know. I laid the groundwork early about what this book is and is not—you knew that if you were looking for a stuffy academic handbook, you were in the wrong place. You could see this related not only to the content but the tone. I'm not talking to you like someone from the world of academia, nor am I using the tone I leaned into for twenty years in my previous HR career.

See what I mean?

I'm guessing as you established your business, you may have done work around developing an ideal client avatar. Maybe you've even done it multiple times as your business has grown, evolved, and undergone pivots. Preparing to write a book like this is much the same.

With this groundwork under your belt, it's easy to ask yourself if you enjoy working with the types of clients you are currently serving. If you don't, digging into who you want to work with is critical before moving forward with writing your book.

If you want to really leverage it for all it's worth and get a great return on investment, you want to focus on what you'll be offering folks down the road…how your book will lead them to a service program or some other paid offering with you. How will you be able to position it as a tie-in for speaking engagements where you want to get booked?

Much of this will show up not only in the flow of your chapters but in the back matter (the pages that come after the body of your book) as well. You'll overtly share how your reader can work with you, and you'll also give them the opportunity to get on your mailing list by opting in to a value-add downloadable or resource.

To help you delve a little deeper in this area specifically as it relates to your audience (aka future clients), here are some questions for you to think about as you develop a reader profile for your book:

- What's their stage of life?
- What problem are they trying to solve?
- What have they tried that's failed them in the past?
- What have they tried and loved but just didn't quite get them across the finish line?
- Where are they in their journey to finding a solution?
- Are they looking for religious/faith-based, spiritual, or pragmatic solutions?

- Is their background and experience more academic based or more real-world experience?

- What other books have they read on the topic you will be writing about?

- What sources other than books do they turn to for solutions?

- What would transformation look like for them?

- What is the next step you want them to take with you after reading your book?

- What might prevent them from taking that step?

- How will you engage with them once they are finished reading your book?

- What else is important to remember about them as you write your book, then invite them to buy it?

As you answer these questions, consider your answers not merely as data points but as intimate details helping you better know that one specific person, the one you'll be having a conversation with as you write—and others like her.

Before we move on, I want to reassure you that narrowing down your focus doesn't mean that no one is going to read your book except those you are *specifically* writing for.

By and large my clients are women—my brand, books, and marketing reflect that. *But* I occasionally work with men too; many find value in the work I produce, including my books.

This is one of those bits of magic we talked about in the early pages of this book. When you focus on who you want to attract—the people you want to connect with—other people will also be drawn to what you create. Yet others will be turned off by it. There is nothing wrong with that; it's a needed realization.

You can't—and aren't meant to—serve everyone. Operating with this knowledge is what allows you to be incredibly good at what you do. It's also what will empower you to write a book that serves a purpose greater than yourself.

Content, tone, and style carry over into our upcoming conversations; knowing your audience dictates all of that. I hope you'll invest some time here before moving on.

CHAPTER HIGHLIGHTS

- Understanding your reader is as important as understanding your customer.
- Knowing your audience guides the content you create—the tone and style of your writing, as well as how you market your book.
- Attracting some people and turning off others is a natural part of the marketing process.

PROFIT WRITE PONDERINGS

1. How does the type of person you are writing for differ from your current clients?

2. What is the most notable aspect of your reader profile?

3. What new discoveries and understanding did you gain in considering your reader?

4. What do you want your reader to do when they finish the book—that is, what are you leading them to?

CHAPTER 7

PLAN THE JOURNEY

Every good book takes a reader on a journey; in the case of the kinds of books we're writing, that journey is helping them get from where they are to where they want to be.

Luckily, you've already done the groundwork that provides you with their starting location by working through the previous chapter. And it's always easier to get to your destination when you know the starting coordinates, right?

As for the destination, we're going to think beyond the book, but we'll take our readers through a process of transformation on the way there. As you get ready to think about this map you'll create, I want you to think less about yourself and more about your reader.

It's not about taking anyone on a journey they feel forced to take but instead about taking them on one they are excited...

joyful…empowered…(insert whatever word best describes how you want them to feel) to embark upon—one they've been waiting to embark on with the right guide to lead them.

Don't lose sight of the fact that your reader is the hero of this story. You will make a genuine connection much faster than you can ever imagine by keeping the spotlight on them, not yourself. Your reader doesn't need to be rescued; they need to be honored and respected. Guiding them to that end is what will make you stand out.

Think about that and reflect on these questions:

After they've read your book…

- What are they celebrating? What have they accomplished? What significant milestones have they reached?
- What have they learned and let go of? Where have their perspectives shifted?
- What do they now have the confidence and courage to do?
- What do they understand in a deeper, more purposeful way?
- What's changed? How is their reality different from when they set out on this journey with you?

Ponder those questions, and then think about what readers will need when they reach that point. And make no mistake: no matter how phenomenal of a book you write, they will still need *something*. In fact, even if your book theoretically had *everything* they needed, they wouldn't be able to access it because they'd get lost or bored in the length, depth, and minutiae of all the details.

Don't be discouraged or defensive here. This is good news.

Your goal is to help readers move forward a step at a time... maybe even help them leapfrog a few steps ahead. But something that is true for all of us: *we don't know what we don't know.*

Your book is going to peel back a new layer of understanding. With that new level of awareness comes the new knowledge of what more they need to get to where they want to go. Heck, through your book they may even realize they've been going in the wrong direction. Maybe their transformation will be in gaining clarity about what they really want.

We're not creating an encyclopedia; we're writing a single book with an overarching message. About one desired destination.

The goal isn't to cram in everything you know—or believe you know—that they'll need at some point.

Our job is to strip away the weight of distractions, all the noise that doesn't matter, and get them to the next waypoint—

without detour. Once you're there, you'll support them with what they need next.

We aren't the ones driving. We are the navigators.

Transformation occurs in varying degrees of intensity. Your goal isn't to control your reader...to take the wheel, so to speak. With each choice you make for this book, remember, you are riding shotgun. You have a different viewpoint of the trip, and you can help them see what you see. You can hang out a bit, and when they want to get back on the road, you might be the one there with them, or you might hand off the role of guide to someone who is better equipped for the next leg of the journey.

Metaphors aside, let's pause and flip the conversation to a business-building perspective.

None of us—even as thought leaders—is the be-all and end-all. We'll be one expert who supports this person over the course of their life as they work to get where they want to go.

We may have an offering—a program, service, digital product, workshop, or class—that will move them on to the next step. This is the place where readers can become clients.

Let's play with that idea for a minute.

For the sake of this example, assume you're a business coach and those you want to work with are mid-level women who have left the corporate world to build an online business. They are at the very beginning stages of their work, and they're in luck, because that's your area of expertise.

You're a wiz at the strategies needed in the start-up phase, and you use your book to help them find solutions to the problems keeping them up at night. As you transition to the end of your book, you lead them to that next step through a resource you provide free access to, accompanied by an email sequence that invites them to work with you.

They become your client.

Well, let me rephrase that.

Of course, not every reader will become a client. Truth is, we don't want them to be. I don't have that kind of bandwidth—and neither do you. Plus, you've earned the right to be selective in who you work with. Just because someone has read your book doesn't automatically mean they are ready to do the work required or to make the investment needed to get to the next level with you. But we do want to give them the opportunity to explore the option.

My intention isn't to take you down a rabbit hole here. There are many more layers of complexities that can be explored. And I know you probably have a solid grasp on business building, but sometimes when you introduce a book into the equation, it can muddy the waters.

My goal here is to simply spark thoughts of what next steps could look like beyond the end of your book—and to engage your thinking in a way that includes how you'll create a book that's another business-building tool at your disposal. Being clear on your strategy will help you more clearly create a book that provides value, supports the reader, and hits the mark as a tool that helps you meet your business goals.

From a planning perspective, here's what the journey you're creating for your reader looks like:

> **Beginning:** They have a problem or pain point that they need to solve, and your book looks like it may help.
>
> **Middle:** You help them develop a new awareness or understanding and experience some level of transformation.
>
> **End:** Their goal feels possible. You've given them enough information to experience an early win. They feel like they can get where they want to go.
>
> **Call to Action:** They feel like they can go further and get there faster with your support. You make an invitation, and they consider working with you in a deeper capacity.

All of this is another layer of the foundation you're building as you prepare to create your book. It will come into play as you begin to craft your outline as described in an upcoming chapter.

CHAPTER HIGHLIGHTS

○ Your book needs to be about your reader, not you.

○ Your reader is the hero of this story; you are the guide.

○ The best-planned journey for your reader solves a problem and sparks transformation.

PROFIT WRITE PONDERINGS

1. What is the main problem of your primary reader that you can solve?

2. What transformation do they desire?

3. How will your book help them get there?

4. What is the next step you'll lead them to after they finish your book?

CHAPTER 8

COMMIT TO CONNECTION

Storytelling

There's one more thing for us to chat about before moving into building and writing mode—being intentional about making a strong connection with your reader as they journey through your book.

Studies show that stories are remembered up to twenty-two times better than facts. Based on that statistic alone, it should go without saying that when you want to explain something, make a point, or demonstrate an idea in a tangible way, storytelling is the way you can best accomplish that. It makes the connection with your reader and makes it stick.

But let's take it one step further. Let's focus on forging a deeper, more meaningful outcome. If your reader can "see" themselves in your story in some way, and if they *feel* emotion, it becomes an even stronger point of connection.

To be clear here, I don't mean trying to manipulate your reader's emotions.

I heard intuitive writing coach Megan Barnhard tell a story recently about being frustrated with how attempts at manipulation have become prevalent on social media. I can't improve on her sentiment. She said, **"When people tell stories from which they didn't learn anything—but they present the stories like they're important and life altering—the storyteller is faking an epiphany like they're faking an orgasm. All for the sake of selling something."**

News flash: people know if we're faking it, and no one likes to be swindled or sold.

It's the sharing of a relevant and authentic story related to the topic or point you're trying to make that creates a bridge to a meaningful emotional-level connection.

It's also important to point out the fact that some stories you most love to tell won't make the cut for your book. This can happen for several reasons, but the ones that should quickly get the red-pen treatment are ones that don't strengthen the point you are trying to make.

Listen, I get the temptation. I'd love to tell you the story about the time I was mistaken for a producer of the *Oprah Winfrey Show* outside Radio City Music Hall in New York City or how I hit the Publish button on my very first (and awful) website on a train ride to an event in Boston or about the full-circle moment of being invited to speak on Jack Canfield's stage, but *none* of those stories are going to serve you—your head, your heart, or my point—right now. (But if we ever meet up at a coffee shop, ask me about *any* of these and I'll gladly share them with you.)

When we have limited time to make a connection with our audience, not only do our stories have to be relevant, but we also want them leaning in, wanting more. Having a collection of stories top of mind that you can choose from makes this process feel much more natural. In the case of books, it's also something that keeps the phenomenon commonly known as writer's block at bay.

The way we can strengthen this skill is through the practice of story banking.

In fact, this process helped me uncover an important story that you may relate to…and one that helped me understand more clearly the root of some of the blocks and fears I personally experienced in the past around putting myself out there as an author—the first time I felt harshly judged for my writing.

I was seventeen and had gotten roped into participating in my first—*and only*—pageant. Beyond swimsuits, gowns, and talent, an element of the competition was an interview with a panel of judges. In preparation for that, we had to write and submit an essay about our career aspirations. For context, this was back in the day…long before the era of spellcheck and tools like Grammarly. I meticulously scoured my work and referenced a dictionary for any word that felt like it had the potential to be misspelled. I had others check my work too. I wanted to make sure everything was *jusssst* right.

When the time finally came to participate in the interview, it felt like things were going well. The conversation was cordial, and my anticipatory nerves had settled. That is, until the last judge spoke.

"I see you want to be a journalist. The problem is that your words and your work don't match up," she said, looking down her nose at me, eyes peering over the top of her glasses.

My brows knit together involuntarily; my head tilted slightly to the left. There was no hiding my confusion.

"Miss Diffin, you will *never* become a journalist, turning in sloppy work like this."

Her words struck like barbs. My face flushed as if seared by the sun, and the room's air seemed to evaporate, leaving a suffocating heat that made me feel like my knees were going to buckle beneath me.

What was surely only seconds felt like hours. My mind was racing as I played out two distinct scenarios in my mind—kind of like those "devil on one shoulder, angel on the other" cartoon depictions, except there were devils on both my shoulders.

Why do you have it out for me? I wanted to ask her. *Show me these so-called mistakes! You have no idea how hard I worked on this stupid essay…and I can prove it.*

It felt like she was gaslighting me, although I had no name for it then.

But just as quickly, my thoughts turned to…

Get the hell out of here…run…hide! You're such an embarrassment. Who do you think you are to do something like this? You have no right to be here. Of course she's calling you out. You're a big fat loser.

The reality of the situation was I didn't act on either thought. Instead, I politely thanked her for her feedback, silently prayed to be dismissed *quickly* before I was embarrassed any further, and with the microscopic shred of dignity I had left, found the closest private space where I discreetly let my tears—and mascara—flow down my face.

Feelings of anger and embarrassment were present, but what I recall most vividly is how devastated I felt. I loved to write. I'd even won some writing contests and awards. But in an instant, every ounce of belief I'd had in myself and my abilities was ripped to shreds like Edward Scissorhands had entered the room, hands flailing.

You may have never participated in a pageant or stood before a judge, but I am willing to bet you know that *feeling*…that kind of humiliation. As you read about this encounter, you might have even felt a knot in your gut, a flash of anger toward that judge, maybe even experienced a bit of empathy because someone made you feel like this in the past. And for a moment, we were connected at a heart level. The root cause may be different, but I have doubts about my writing just like you.

I have well over a hundred other stories in my story bank that won't make their way to this book, but they'll serve another purpose. Had I not gone through the process of mining for story ideas, I never would have accessed this particular one as having any value. It's embarrassing, after all. But it's the perfect story to demonstrate this point. It also created a spark that helped me access other memories that I added to my bank for future use.

Story Banks

A story bank is sorta like a treasure chest; there is always something of value for you to find there. So let's start to build yours up, shall we?

There are so many ways you can access the gold mine of your personal stories. I'm going to share a couple here, but I also have a free downloadable for you containing 101 prompts to help you access those gems. (You can access it using the QR code in the Resource Roundup section at the back of the book.)

One way to get started is to think about your life in a chronological way—think in terms of a timeline.

What memories/stories stand out to you from your early childhood? Then what about junior high and high school? College? Early adulthood? Before marriage? Before kids? After each of those? First job, last job, worst job? You get the idea. The most important thing about this exercise is that you go into it without any judgment. Refrain from putting limits on what ends up on your list. Those things where you might say, "I would never tell that story"? Include those too. You'll have control over how you use them, and the simple act of writing them down might spark another story you want to use.

Another less linear way to start mining stories is to think in categories—like personal life lessons, embarrassing moments (like showing up for an interview to find that your suit matches the upholstery of the waiting room chairs...Ask me how I know! *insert face palm*), accomplishments, disappointments—and the stories associated with each.

With both approaches, you'll record a sentence or two about the story—just enough so *you* will remember what you need and want to. It's not about fully writing it out to document the whole story; it's simply the basis of the story you'll want to capture.

Observation: it's funny how our minds work sometimes.

My client Angela was crafting an email to send to let me know she didn't think this "story bank thing" was going to work for her. As she continued with her argument, a story—a really important one related to her business origin—came to mind almost as if it was some sort of magic.

She still sent the note and let me know about the story idea she accessed while writing the email. Then she was off to the races. That one recollection unlocked a series of stories—some that will make the cut for her book, others that will be used on blogs, newsletters, social posts, and in a variety of other ways. She doesn't know how she will use each of them right now, but she does see the value of doing this prework and continuing the practice as time goes on. Bottom line: the time you invest in getting the right stories onto the page will pay big dividends, in both the writing process and the genuine, trusting relationship you build with your reader, and carry over to postlaunch outcomes.

CHAPTER HIGHLIGHTS

- Stories help readers remember important points.
- Authentic stories build connection; faking significance damages the relationship.
- Not all stories belong in your book.
- Creating a story bank will help you more easily access the right ones.

PROFIT WRITE PONDERINGS

1. Which stories do you tell often that you think should make their way into your book? Which serve a better purpose elsewhere?

2. What personal stories do you shy away from because it feels vulnerable to share them even though they could serve your audience on a deep level?

3. When was the last time you moved stories from your head to an actual story-bank document?

4. What's one strategy for accessing stories that you'll dedicate time to?

PART III

TIME TO BUILD

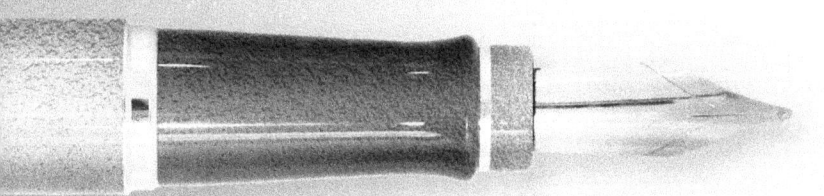

CHAPTER 9

CREATE YOUR OUTLINE

Before we begin this section, I want to take a quick time-out for a big bravo and high five to you for not skipping over this chapter. I know outlines are not sexy, but man, does a good one make a world of difference when it comes to writing—or more specifically, *finishing*—your book.

That said, I've gotta come clean. When I got the idea for this book, it came fast and furious. I started writing to capture all my thoughts. That is, until it occurred to me I was falling into the same trap I help others avoid...the one that keeps so many people from finishing their books: writing without a plan.

I don't have any secret superpowers that remove the temptation to fly by the seat of my pants and write without direction. The only thing that saved me here is that I recognized what I was doing. And honestly, I had to laugh at myself. After all, how ridiculous—and at the same time, divinely perfect.

It gave me a better understanding of how this happens, and it reminded me that often it's passion and enthusiasm, not impatience, that lead people to skip the outlining step. But that's not the only reason they do.

I've had people share lots of reasons why they don't create outlines. Can you see yourself in any of these?

- "Outlines are too rigid."
- "The process of planning takes the joy out of writing."
- "I trust that whatever I write is what I'm meant to write."
- "I have to write the minute I have the idea or else I'll forget it."
- "The act of writing is what helps me figure out what comes next."
- "I know what I'm going to write. I don't need to waste time on an outline."

Truth is, some of these things may have a shred of validity when it comes to *starting* a book, but it's *finishing* the book that I'm more concerned about—for me, for you, and for those I coach.

That's why I'm laying out an overview of my Killer Outline process for you here. You'll see it doesn't have to be rigid and confining; rather, it will be the guide that keeps you on track while still allowing for creativity and fun. Plus, you'll get a clearer understanding of the steps I've led you through in the previous chapters, which is foundational to this work.

All the combined elements we've talked about are a huge factor in allowing you to write quickly. You've invested the needed time in preparing so that when it's time to write, the words flow from you with ease. There are still some steps after this to round out the system, but let's focus on the outline for now.

Going into this process we've already narrowed down who you are writing for and the journey you're going to take them on in parts 1 and 2. Now, here in part 3, think of the Killer Outline as the detailed map with waypoints to pull everything together in one place. It's a reference…something concrete to come back to every time you sit down to write. Unlike traditional outline writing, the process is rarely linear. It requires a good old-fashioned brain dump—one you sift and sort through but will ultimately include everything you need to finish your book without any extra parts or loose ideas.

Step One

What are the main things your reader needs to know? Think high-level topics here and remember this is a brainstorm. You'll popcorn out ideas. We know that not everything will make the book, but it doesn't mean it's a bad idea; it's simply better suited for another use.

Step Two

Once you've dumped out all your ideas, it's time to extract the pieces that will systematically lead your reader on the journey they've signed up for by buying your book:

- What do they need to know first?
- Then what?
- What comes after that?

You see where I'm going here, right?

Each of these high-level steps/topics will turn into chapters. Remember, chapters aren't silos. Consider these questions:

- How do they flow together?
- How are they interconnected?
- What's the easiest path to get where you're going without a detour?

Step Three

Once you have these main points fleshed out, it's time to go back in with details. This is the part where we can underestimate the power of documenting our thinking. Once we have the chapters mapped, our minds trick us into believing we'll remember everything that led us to these decisions and all the details we want to include. Sadly, this isn't true.

That's why front-loading the time it takes to tuck in all the relevant pieces now is so important. It releases the mental load of decision-making while writing.

So, what are the details I'm talking about? They will vary from book to book and author to author, but you'll want to include things like these:

- Any statistics relevant to your point
- Stories that will help your audience understand how things apply to them
- Case studies that further support the message you are trying to convey
- Useful tools and/or resources you want to reference
- Reflection questions that might be useful

This stage of the Killer Outline is for you. It won't look like a table of contents but more like an in-process blueprint. You don't need to write in full sentences or in paragraph form here. Record each relevant bit as bullets with just enough detail to tickle your brain. This acts as a reminder about what you're writing next without having to sift through the worry and self-doubt that it leads anywhere.

One of the ways I like to navigate this whole process is with sticky notes, because they provide a great visual while also being easy to move around. I like to color-code and use different-size notes for different elements. Many of my clients do too. None more effectively than my client Tamika—a textbook case of someone who takes her colorful sticky note Killer Outline with her *evvv-err-eeee-where.*

Tamika is frequently on a plane traveling for work or adventure and has mastered the art of setting up and working from a mobile office. It's always fun to see her posts from exotic locations and get a glimpse of her outline hanging on a wall. Her commitment to writing is made easier by having this easily movable, large but compact outline to review at the start of each writing session, no matter her location.

You might use the notes in different ways, or you might be like my client Angela. The first time she saw a photo of my outline in process, she said the "chaos" of the sticky notes made her head hurt.

This is the beauty of the Killer Outline process. Not that it makes you want to reach for headache medicine but that you can adapt it in the way that works best for you, be it a mind map, a Word doc, or a rainbow collection of sticky notes. It's not about *how* you get it done, it's that you get there in a way that works for you. This is that part where we take the idea of the need for rigidity and throw it out the window.

As you get all of this together, you'll be able to more easily and thoughtfully begin to see the flow your book will take. This allows you to make decisions about organization and structure...to think about how to remove as many barriers—and as much friction—as possible for your reader.

The fine-tuning of getting to organization, structure, and flow will then allow you to go back and create your table of contents, to come up with working titles for each section/chapter that are enticing and purposeful to the content and overall message of your book.

How you choose to do this will vary, depending on your style and tone. I like to use chapter titles that evoke action. When you read through the table of contents, I want it to tell a mini-story or message of its own—something that draws people in. For others, funny—or *punny*—chapter titles work well *if* they match the tone of the overall style of the book. There is not an exact science here, but this step does require intention.

Before we move on to the next chapter, I think it's important to address the amount of time it will take to create your Killer Outline. I wish I could give you specifics, but the answer isn't a black-and-white one. What I can tell you is that those who work with me at intensives spend two full days working through this process and getting everything mapped out for their outline. (Naming the chapters and sections comes later.) For those who work through this part on their own but with coaching support, it typically takes three or four weeks because of their very full schedules, but with dedicated time and discipline it can happen much faster.

While I can't pinpoint the exact amount of time you should spend doing this, I can give you a few very specific bits of guidance that are critical:

1. **Do the prework** (the stuff covered in the first two sections of this book) before diving into the outline.

2. **Don't rush the process.** I'm not suggesting letting it drag on, nitpicking for weeks, but rather to schedule enough time to be thorough. This is what you'll rely on once you start writing. If you haven't done a solid job here, you're not going to get to the finish line with even the bones of a great book.

3. **Allow yourself white space**—time to step away from the work. (It's so important, I even build this into intensives.) When you return to it, you'll have a new perspective. Sometimes it will reveal an area where you aren't even sure what you meant from reading your notes (good to identify now and address!), or something might jump out at you as belonging in a different place in your outline to maintain flow for your reader.

If we aren't able to work together one-on-one and you're feeling like you need more guidance in this area, my Killer Outline mini-course may be the needle mover you need. Check the Resource Roundup page at the end of the book for more information.

CHAPTER HIGHLIGHTS

- Outlines are more about *finishing* your book than starting it.

- Creating your outline systematically doesn't require a rigid, linear process.

- Focus on the outcome, then use the system or method best suited to you to get there.

- Create a structure that takes your reader on a well-thought-out journey.

- Allow yourself adequate time and support for this part of your book creation.

PROFIT WRITE PONDERINGS

1. What is the journey you want to take your reader on?

2. What organizational tools/processes work best for you?

3. What time will you dedicate to creating your outline?

4. What, if any, support do you need to complete your Killer Outline?

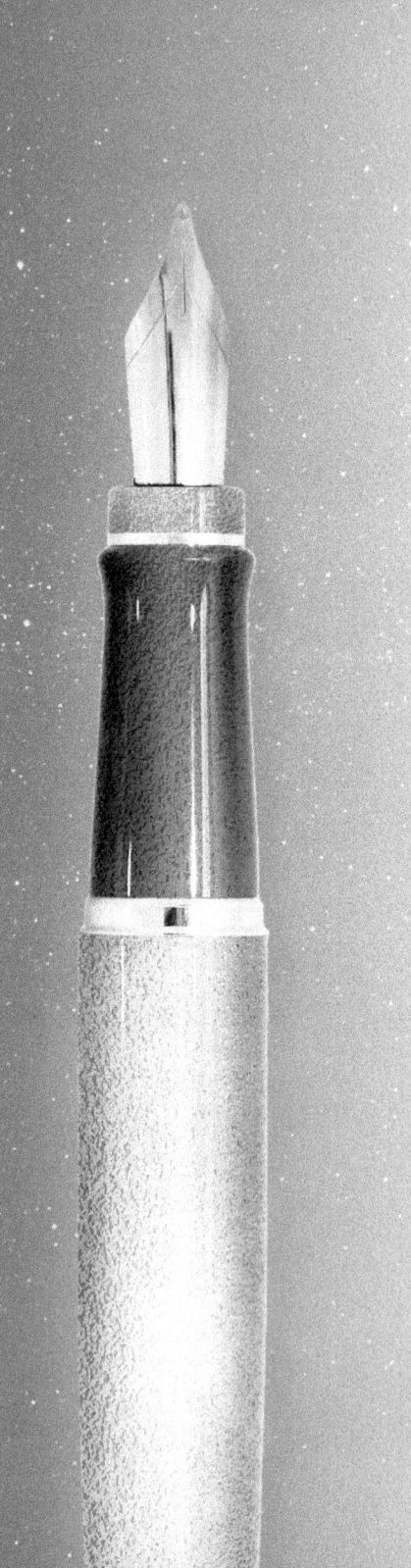

CHAPTER 10

HATCH A PLAN

With your Killer Outline in hand, you've got the green light to start writing. And while that's cool—and somewhat exhilarating—actually carving out time to write can present its own set of challenges, especially for business owners like us juggling multiple priorities in our personal and professional lives. So, let's take care not to leave this to chance.

You don't have to be in my sphere long to know I'm always down for a good celebration and encourage them frequently. This stage is no different, *and* we also need to keep our eye on the ball of creating the book that will grow our business, brand, and impact. That means we've got to get even more tactical here. I don't want you to get lost in the weeds, so I'm going to keep this relatively high level.

Knowing that life happens to all of us, there is no foolproof formula, but I'm going to share a couple of ways you can approach this. First, though, a point worth mentioning:

Word count is going to be the measure we use in calculating how much time you need to schedule for writing. We use that not because it's perfect but because it's a solid starting point.

Getting this to work for you means taking a beat to think about the book you're creating.

You don't need an enormous word count to make a deeply powerful impact. You may be able to look to your personal bookshelf to verify that; I know I can.

The Gifts of Imperfection by Brené Brown, *The Big Leap* by Gay Hendricks, *The Four Agreements* by Don Miguel Ruiz, and *The 12 Week Year* by Brian P. Moran and Michael Lennington are all on my shelf and around 200 pages or less.

If that's the length you are imagining your book to be, you could estimate by working the upcoming calculations using 35,000 words as your base number. Your actual project may be more or less, depending on a few factors, including trim size (the physical size of your book) and the layout design features, but this will give you a basic idea.

Based on 35,000 (for example's sake), we'd divide by twelve weeks—the amount of time in which I encourage new authors to complete their first draft. (More on the *why* behind this in just a bit.)

So, for some quick math, here's what it might look like:

35,000 words ÷ 12 weeks = 2,917 words per week

Then we'd take the words per week and divide by the number of hours you could commit to writing each week. Let's use a conservative number—say, three writing sessions of one hour each.

2,917 words ÷ 3 hours = 972(ish) words per session

In this example, you could equate each session to creating a piece of intentional writing that's a little over the length of an average blog post. Feel doable?

Some weeks it may, others it may not. Using the calculation above to inform your goal setting into a "good, better, best" or "floor and ceiling" type of format may help you keep forward momentum even during weeks that are more challenging.

Good/Better/Best based on the calculation above might look like this:

> Good = 725 words (shy of your original goal but still good progress)
>
> Better = 850 words (closer to your original goal)
>
> Best = 975 words (slightly more than what the calculation alone would have set out for you)

Floor and Ceiling Goals could land somewhere like this:

Floor = 100 words

The floor is your no-matter-what commitment…Imagine having a horrendous day and feeling the lowest of low. A hundred words may be far from where you wanted to be, but it matches the circumstances, and some progress is always better than no progress. It confirms (for your subconscious mind) your commitment to the project regardless of what's going on.

Ceiling = 1,000 words

The ceiling represents that knock-it-out-of-the-park-type day when you are on fire and nothing is getting in your way.

Most days you'll fall somewhere in between the floor and the ceiling, but no matter what, you can celebrate keeping your writing commitment to yourself.

The key to this step in your writing journey is to know yourself, consider your current reality, and be flexible. The word count and goal strategy aren't static—just as the demands of your life and business ebb and flow, so will the amount of time you invest in your book each week. Review your progress weekly and adjust accordingly. This is not the time to stick your head in the sand.

I know it can be tempting to think about setting writing goals just in terms of completing sections or chapters of your book. That works for some people, but if this is your first time writing a full-length book, I recommend the word count calculation—at least through the first half of your book—to get a much more predictable outcome.

Before moving our conversation on to the actual writing part, it is worth sharing again the reason this all works so predictably. It's because you've invested all the time up front that you know the words that flow through your fingertips to your keyboard are going to be intentional. They have a specific purpose. You're not writing for the sake of writing. You're anchored into the journey, the transformation, and the positive outcomes it will create—for your reader and for you.

One final thing before we move on: I want to circle back to the ninety-days recommendation I made earlier in the chapter.

The reason I recommend setting the goal to complete the first draft within this time frame goes back to some of the things we talked about in part 1. The longer we give ourselves to get our first draft across the finish line, the more cracks we leave for all the nagging negative thoughts to creep in, requiring much more intense focus on the mindset work.

CHAPTER HIGHLIGHTS

○ Word count is an effective measure for basing your writing goals.

○ There are several goal-setting approaches; pick what works best for you.

○ Goals and progress may vary from week to week, which is A-OK, but remember to stay anchored into the big picture to keep making progress.

○ Ninety days is a good starting point on which to base your writing goals.

PROFIT WRITE PONDERINGS

1. What's your inspiration book for size and length?

2. On average, how many hours each week do you think you can commit to book writing?

3. Which of the goal-setting strategies from this chapter best suit your personality and preferences?

4. Using the formula given, how many words will you commit to completing during each session?

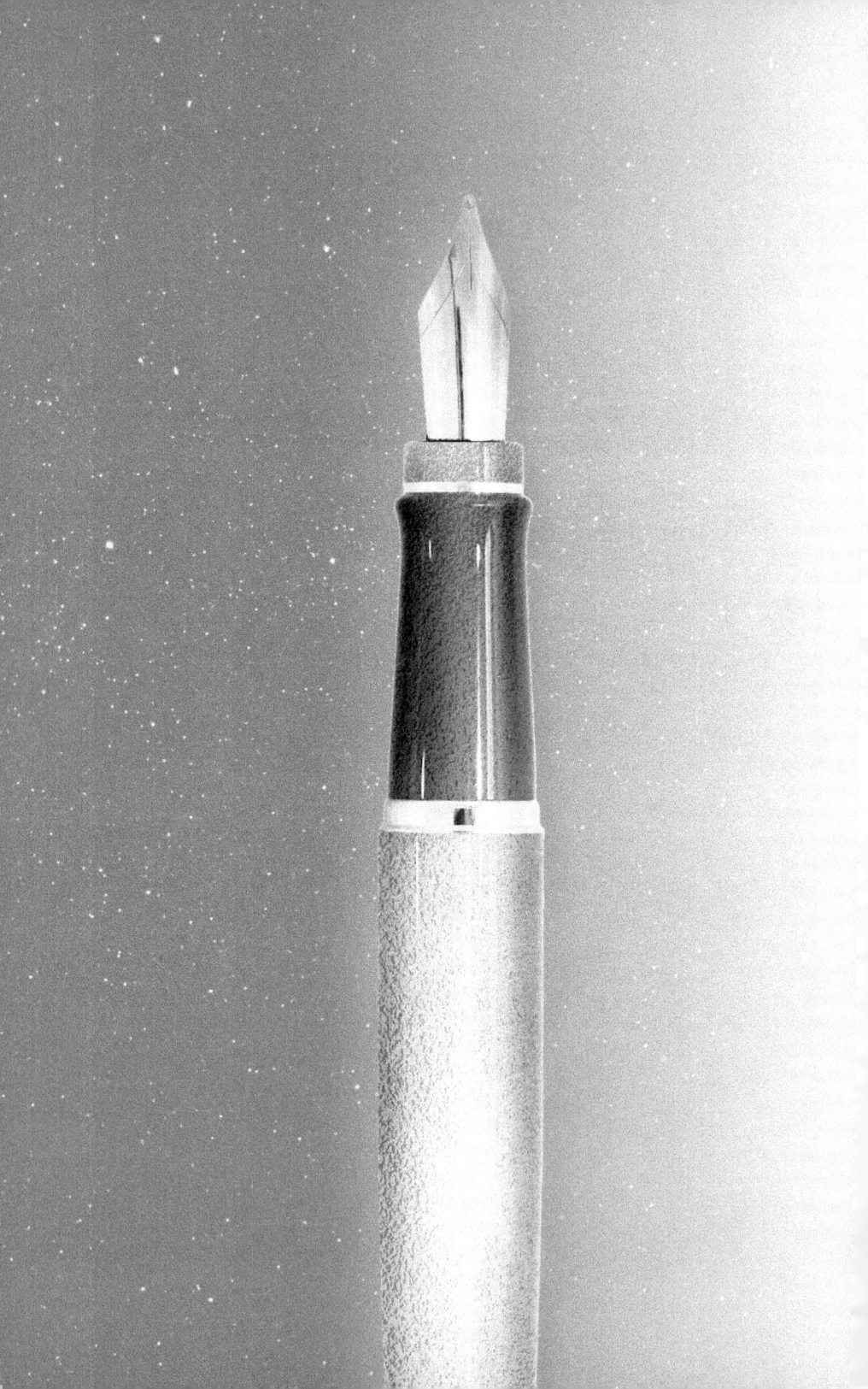

CHAPTER 11

CELEBRATE THE MESS

As I mentioned back in chapter 1, the road to creating your book is going to be messy. I know you may not like the sound of that—maybe even hoped we'd not talk about it again—but here I am, poking that sore spot.

I know we're talking about your book here, but indulge me as I take a slight side step. I promise, you'll see how it relates to your writing shortly.

For a moment, I want you to think about a time you've cleaned out your closet or office, or one of your kids has cleaned their bedroom. These scenarios tend to have a couple of things in common:

1. A tidy environment is the goal.

2. The mess typically gets worse before it gets better.

In my world, even though my husband knows very well what's going on when he sees it, I still find myself explaining the stage I'm in:

- It was a mess before.

- Now it's *really* messy (because it's not just the surface mess, it's drawers, files, and ever-y-thing strewn ever-y-where!).

- In a little while, things will look better than ever!

This is an exact parallel to writing and book creation.

It is a mess—when it's a bunch of thoughts sitting tangled in your mind.

Then it gets really messy—when you start working on your outline…going from a bunch of ideas to bullet points to stories, chapters, and a whole book without editing.

But in a little while, it'll look better than ever—after you edit, refine, and bring in another set of eyes to help.

If you're the type of person who would clean your house before having a housekeeper come in to clean (you know who you are), let's acknowledge that we're getting into territory that is going to stretch you in a new way.

It's a place where you may have to give extra attention to the mindset work we laid out early on. If you've ever worked through your tendency to be a perfectionist, you can almost bet on the fact that it's going to reappear.

The reason for sharing this isn't to scare or discourage you; it's simply to let you know that if it shows up, breathe easy. It's an indication you are on the right track.

Yes, you invested good time in creating your outline, so you are writing with intention. And it will *still* be messy.

It's not going to *stay* messy, and you are going to invite someone in to help you clean it up, but that comes later (stay tuned). Just know that all great books start with a messy first draft.

All those books you see on your bookshelves have gone through a lot of refinement. Don't hold their finished state up as a measuring stick for how your draft should look.

Here's another way to reframe it:

My book matters so much that I will allow it to be bad so it can become good (messy first draft). Then, I'll let it be "good enough" so it can become great (stop self-editing and move it to the hands of your copy editor).

As we close this chapter, I'm going to leave you with a little mantra:

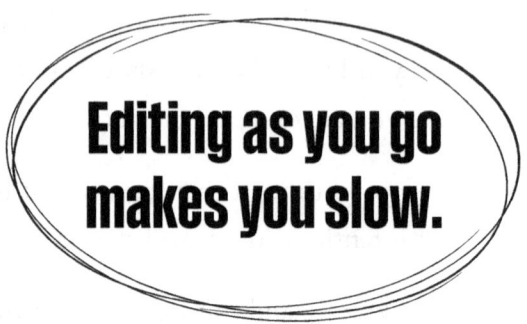

Post it near your writing desk.

Repeat it often.

Maybe even make a voice recording so you can listen to it if you need a reminder.

Our goal is to be sure everything you need to get out onto the page makes its way there. It doesn't have to be pretty yet. Your only job at this stage is to release it from your head to the page.

Once you have a completed manuscript—no matter how messy—*then* you can get to the refinement stage. You literally can't do that if it is floating around in your brain—tangled up with your grocery list and other mundane things you are trying not to forget.

When it's messily on paper or your Word doc, you can enlist the additional support we'll talk about next. No one knows your lived experience, has your knowledge, or can access your intellectual property until you make it available for them to *see*—not just hear about in abstract concept form, but as an actual document.

CHAPTER HIGHLIGHTS

- A mess always precedes a masterpiece.
- Resist the urge to edit as you write.
- "Editing as you go makes you slow."
- The goal of your first draft is simply to get your thoughts out of your head and onto the page (following the outline you created).
- Refinement comes after completion.

PROFIT WRITE PONDERINGS

1. Knowing yourself, how challenging do you think it will be to embrace the messy first draft process?

2. What feelings and emotions does it bring up when you think about delaying the editing process until you have a completed draft?

3. What extra mindset work may be required for you to embrace the mess?

4. What tools, techniques, and strategies will you have on hand to support yourself through the process?

CHAPTER 12

ADD THE SPARKLE AND SHINE

Now that everything rolling around in your brain has made it out onto the page and you've completed that messy first draft, it's time to add the sparkle and shine. Just like with the tumbled sea glass I find on the beaches here on the coast of Maine or polished gemstones you find in the jewelry store, this process will take more than one pass. It will also include more eyes to see—and hands to handle—it.

Getting bogged down here is what we want to avoid at all costs, so it is helpful to think about it as three main phases:

- Self-Editing
- Alpha Reader Feedback
- Professional Copy Editing

Let's start with the self-editing process. It's where you begin to clean things up—the obvious clutter but then even more. I suspect you'll be chomping at the bit to dig into this, but I do have to share a word of caution: don't dive into this too quickly. Having a bit of time and space away from the writing and the work provides a fresh new perspective from which you can view everything:

- You'll notice the places where your thoughts wander and leave people hanging.

- You'll pick up on the places where you repeat a particular phase a few times too many.

- You'll discover where you made assumptions about what your reader knows and recognize where you may need to spell things out in a bit more detail.

- And of course, there's all that grammar-type stuff you'll see and be able to fix too.

The self-editing process intermingles with the other editing phases, but for now—in the first pass—those are the kinds of things you'll be looking for and find.

The next step is enlisting alpha readers—the first outside eyes that see your manuscript. For many authors, sharing their early, messy writing with people they respect feels like a big leap into vulnerability, so I'm imagining this may be what you're thinking too.

But you're not handing off your work to just anyone and simply asking for feedback. Engaging alpha readers is about tapping into the insights of a handful of people who play a specific role *and* giving them a very specific set of instructions as they review your work.

You aren't looking for grammar and sentence structure kinds of refinement, and you'll let them know that right up front. The person who cannot help correcting the grammar on your Facebook posts is not the person you want looking at your work at this stage. (We *all* know someone like that, right?) They'll understand your manuscript is unedited and will likely have those kinds of issues. They can be most helpful by providing answers to questions like these:

- Which sections resonated with you the most?
- Where did you need more information or find the content unclear?
- Were there any parts where your interest started to wane?
- Did you come across any material that seemed out of place?
- What was your overarching takeaway from the book?

You can probably see how this feedback would be much more useful than hearing that you have a run-on sentence or used too many exclamation points!

That doesn't mean these things won't get addressed; it just means that at this early stage, it's not where your focus needs to be. You'll pick up errors, but more importantly, your copy editor is going to make you look like a grammar rock star when they get their hands on your manuscript. The feedback you receive from your alpha readers is to help you tighten up the structure and flow of your manuscript before handing it off for editing.

Now, let me be clear. Even when you give people specific instructions and questions to answer, you're not going to act on all the feedback you receive. Typically, three to five people are going to play this role for you, and what you'll be looking for is overlap and themes in their responses. Plus, you're going to put everything through the filter of your vision and goals for the book.

To get the most useful feedback, you'll want to invite a mix of people to be alpha readers for you:

- Someone who would consider your ideal reader
- Someone who has experience with your genre or topic or book writing in general
- Someone who has knowledge of your topic area
- Someone who would be in your general audience but not have much knowledge of your topic

Notice your best friend and your favorite aunt aren't on this list? They may fit into one of those categories, but be thoughtful in your selections. As warm and fuzzy as the affirmation of doing a good job feels, your goal at this stage is to get useful feedback to help you refine your work.

For the record, while an honest assessment is what you are looking for, you don't want to pick someone who is overly critical by nature, either.

Selecting people you respect allows the critical feedback to land differently. You know they aren't trying to tear you down. They are sharing simply from a perspective of helping you do your best work.

Inviting the right people is a balancing act, but it's worth the effort.

Once you've gotten the feedback and considered what you'll act on, you'll make your edits to create a solid first draft.

So, let's review where you are before handing your manuscript over to a copy editor:

- You've done it messy.
- You did some tidying.
- You've asked for feedback.
- You've completed early editing.

Why go to so much trouble if you're going to hand it off to a professional for editing? Frankly, it matters to your bottom line. The dollars and cents of it is that the better shape your writing is in before you hand it off, the fewer revisions and number of editing passes will be needed to get your manuscript into print-ready shape. This all equates to time and money savings.

Simply stated, it's another place to think about profitability.

Before we move on from this chapter, I want to make a special mention about choosing the copy editor you work with, because it's a choice that will have a huge influence on your book experience. I believe if you're reading this, you have more than one book in you, so having a good experience with your first book makes it much more likely you'll continue with sharing more of your brilliance in book form in the future. (I know...let's get your first book written before we start talking about others.)

Having a relationship that feels like a partnership, not like you're at the mercy of an uptight-red-pen-wielding-antagonist-eager-to-find-your-mistakes-so-she-can-tear-you-down kind of person, is critical.

The copy editor I work with most often and frequently recommend to clients is recognizably invested in every project she takes on. She isn't going through the technical motions, and it doesn't feel transactional. She provides guidance and feedback that honors the voice and brilliance of the author.

She's thoughtful and makes suggestions for consideration around how to make their work clearer or give it that little extra bit of shine, but through more of a dialogue than something strictly instructive.

As you move into this phase, ask around and get recommendations from friends and colleagues. But also interview those you are considering hiring. Communication styles, timelines, and a host of other things can impact the suitability of a good match for your copy editor just as with any hire in your business.

CHAPTER HIGHLIGHTS

- Give yourself some time and space away from your completed messy first draft before jumping into the editing phase.
- Investing time in the pre-professional editing phases impacts not only the quality of your book but also your bottom line.
- Give careful consideration to those you invite to be your alpha readers.
- Provide clear instructions and guidance to alpha readers to get the most useful feedback.
- Choose a professional copy editor who communicates in a way that fits your preferred style.

PROFIT WRITE PONDERINGS

1. Whom will you consider asking to be your alpha readers?

2. Whom can you ask about copy editor recommendations?

3. What feels important to you as it relates to the communication style of the alpha readers and copy editor you choose?

PART IV

PREPARE TO RISE

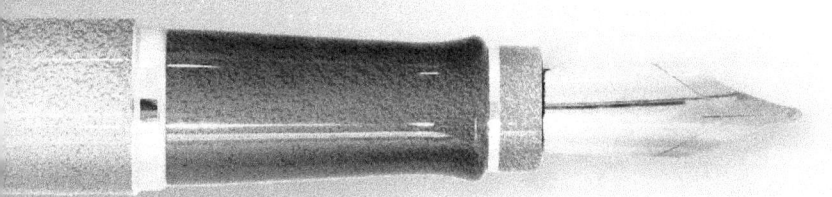

CHAPTER 13

RAISE YOUR VISIBILITY

In this stage, you will wrap up the writing elements of your book and your manuscript will be moving into the hands of your production team. We'll get into publishing and launching, but before we do, it's important that you're not in hiding mode. Let's continue the conversation we started at the beginning of this book about visibility—about your willingness to be seen.

Ideally you'll take my early directive in chapter 4 to heart and share your book journey from the moment you begin to write, pulling back the curtain on the process and dripping out teasers of what is to come. If you do, it will make the elevation of your visibility, and that of your book, a whole lot easier. If you find yourself in a place of nearing publication and have been as quiet as a mouse, you can't change that. What's past is past. But what you can do is make a commitment to show up from this point forward.

Your original motivations for creating a book were around profitability and impact, right? The simple truth is that both of those things require you to let people know you have something that is beneficial for them, something that will alleviate their pain or make their life or business better in some way.

You can do this by offering peeks into your book like…

- sharing your reasons and motivation for writing it,
- excerpts or quotes, and
- audio recordings of you reading a passage or a specific story from the book.

Simultaneously, you'll want to continue sharing your journey with people on your social media channels:

- Share the stage of creation you're in (hired a copy editor, final round of edits, cover and layout design, and so on).
- Share a challenge you've overcome and/or lessons you've learned about yourself in the process.
- Share why you're writing the book, whom it's for, and how it can help.

- Share your emotions as you near publication (It's getting real, folks!).

- Share what's coming...that you'll be inviting them to join the launch team.

If you choose to poll your audience and involve them in making choices, such as...

- voting on cover design options;

- polling them about naming, like which subtitle most resonates with them; and

- soliciting opinions about interior design elements...

...know that all of this is subjective opinion. Your ideal readers typically won't have the knowledge about search engine optimization, color psychology, and genre norms that your book team has, so you'll want to weigh this feedback carefully. It won't always result in changing your initial plan, but sometimes you'll glean great insights you can pass on to your team that will shape an expanded or revised vision of the physical appearance of your book.

The purpose of all this is to keep your book top of mind...to give your future readers a chance to feel like they've helped you and become even more invested in your/your book's success and for your champions to be ready to join your launch team. (We'll be talking about that later in this section.)

All this is a solid start, but you'll want to go further, to begin being seen by people who don't already know you. Leveraging other people's platforms is a great way to accomplish this.

What do I mean by platforms? Basically, communities of people like your ideal reader built by other people in the form of podcasts, summits, magazines, YouTube, and other social media channels.

The really good news is that because of the work we did early on, you're already in tune with your future readers, so it will be easy to know what platforms will be a great fit. If the reader you're trying to reach spends most of their time on social media hanging out on TikTok, then doing a LinkedIn live interview isn't going to get you the most bang for your buck when it comes to time investment. Likewise, if they don't listen to podcasts but do read blogs and articles, that's a great indicator of where to start.

Notice I'm talking about your *reader* here, not *you*.

You might be more comfortable writing a guest article for your favorite blog than recording a podcast (because you aren't in love with your voice) or being on video or TV (because you have some false narrative floating around in your head about not looking good on camera), but if your reader isn't into blogs, you're wasting your energy. You'll feel like you're taking action but be disappointed in the outcome it produces, because it's not of the needle-moving variety that includes your desired readers.

My big hang-up in this area was anything that was airing live. Because of that experience I told you about earlier—with the pageant judge—and an accumulation of other confidence-rocking moments, I held on to a lot of insecurities.

I had a fear of stepping into a looming "Gotcha" moment where someone would inevitably ask me a trick question or something I didn't know or turn around what I said to mean something other than what I intended.

What I've come to learn is that anyone who has you on their show wants you to succeed…They *want* you to do well (barring places like the *Maury Povich Show*—yes, I'm dating myself—but that isn't the kind of show we're aiming for).

Truth is, it makes for a better experience for the host's audience and makes it more likely that other people will want to be a guest on their show too. That is certainly the case for me when I'm wearing my podcast host hat.

After vetting potential guests to make sure they are a good fit for my *She Gets Published* podcast audience and extending an invitation to join me, my goal becomes creating an experience that is valuable to both my listeners *and* my guests. I want to help them shine!

All this being said, I'd be lying if I said I no longer get nervous when I get invited or pitch for interviews or guest appearances that feel like particularly high-stakes opportunities. I have to remind myself that it feels this way because I'm on my growth edge and this chance matters to me.

I prepare.
I show up.
I do my best.
I provide value.
I learn.
I move on.

If you're reading all this and practically breaking out in hives just thinking about being in the spotlight, a good resource for you is Linda Ugelow's book, *Delight in the Limelight*.

Visibility is something to come to terms with in all aspects of your business. I could go on here (the business strategist in me is just chomping at the bit to go deeper), but let's keep it directed toward your book right now.

You'll maximize each of these opportunities to get in front of an audience by including things in your bio and/or weaving information into your interview answers that highlights the fact that you have a book coming out on this topic. You can include a line in your bio that says something like, "author of the forthcoming book *xyz*," or "author of *xyz*—available fall 20xx."

You can strategically reference your book when answering a question. It doesn't have to be overt to be effective. Subtle is fine—just get it out into the world by speaking the name of your book.

To bring this chapter to a close, but also to put an exclamation point on it, I want you to start thinking about visibility and being seen like the infinity symbol—it never ends. You don't have to be "on" all hours of the day and night, but you do need to be intentional about showing up on a consistent basis. It not only puts you forward as a leader/expert on your topic but also creates content that you can repurpose and use in a way that has people telling you, "I'm seeing you everywhere!"

As Jen Gottlieb, author of the bestselling book *Be Seen*, reminds us: ***"Visibility is your responsibility."*** (If you don't have her book yet, grab it!)

It's not about being seen for the sake of being seen. It's showing up in service of your future reader. If they don't know about you and your book, you can't help them. And what a crying shame that would be—especially after all the love and care you poured into creating this book for them.

CHAPTER HIGHLIGHTS

- Your willingness to be "seen" is key to your book's success.

- Share sneak peeks into your creation process and the book's content.

- Leverage other people's platforms to increase your visibility and reach a larger audience.

- Be present in the places where your ideal reader hangs out rather than just the places you prefer.

PROFIT WRITE PONDERINGS

1. What hang-ups do you still have about being seen? (Dig deep and get really honest with yourself here.)

2. What steps will you take to reframe any negative thoughts you still have around visibility?

3. Which social platforms are your readers most active on?

4. What podcasts, blogs, and shows do your readers subscribe to, and which ones would be a good match as a place for you to be seen?

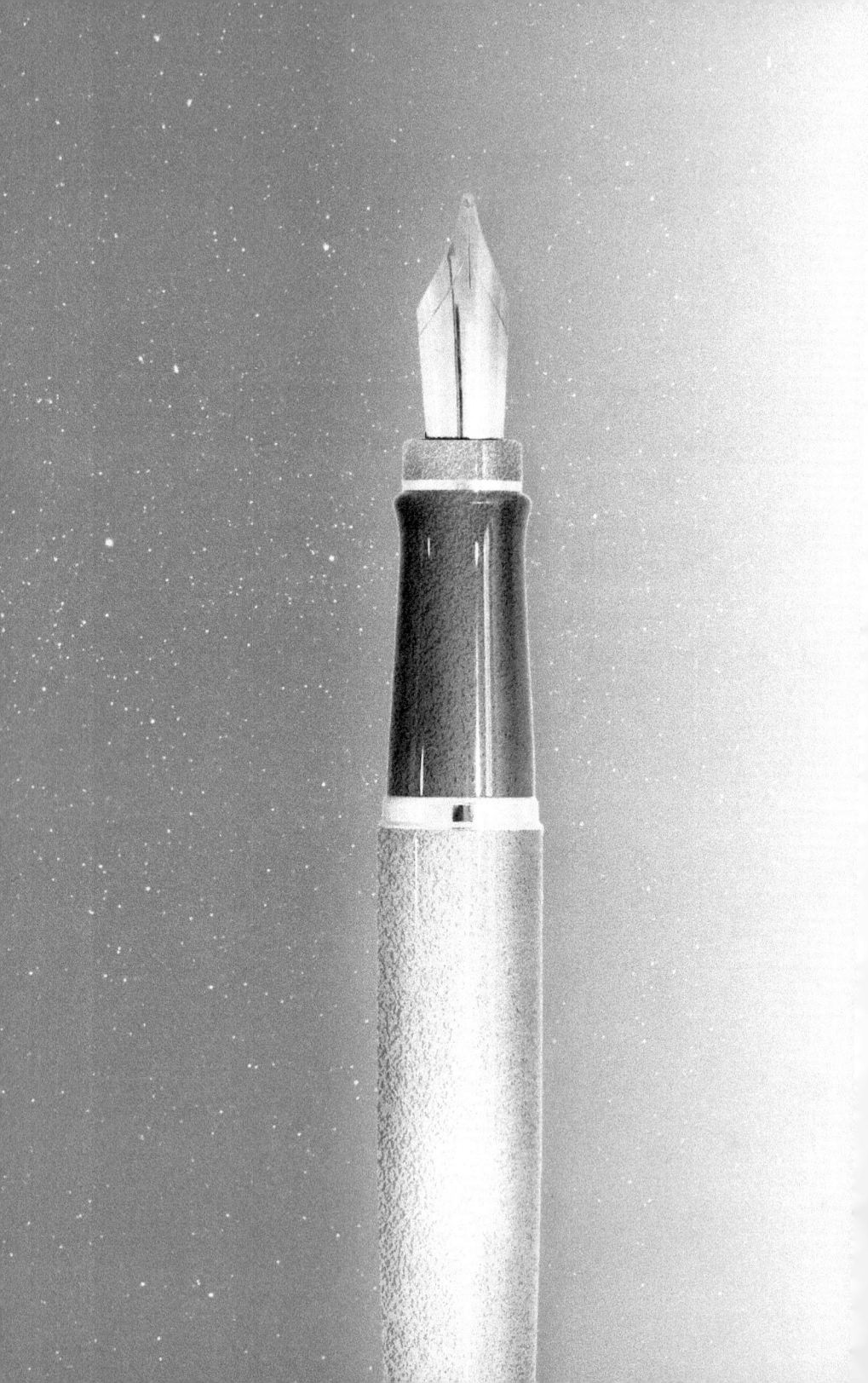

CHAPTER 14

DECIDE AND PUBLISH

Let's start by stating the obvious:

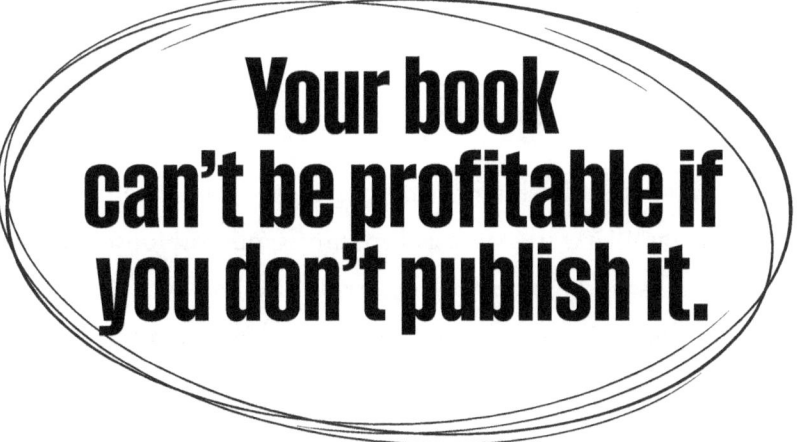

Don't stall out now.

The publishing industry is changing at warp speed, and while it can be tough to keep up, it's not all bad. Many of the changes are making the process accessible to more people. Not only that, but they're also allowing for faster entry into the market.

At the time I'm writing this for you, there are three main routes to getting your book published—traditional, hybrid, and self-publishing. All of them serve a purpose and provide their own set of benefits. The route you choose will be dictated by your goals.

I'm going to give you a glimpse of them all, but in full disclosure, I do have a bias toward professional self-publishing; it's the route I most often recommend and have firsthand experience with, both as an author and in mentoring my clients. (The book you're holding in your hands right now is self-published.)

Traditional Publishing

Traditional publishing houses are those you are most likely to be familiar with, such as Penguin/Random House, HarperCollins, and Simon & Schuster. Typically, if you are signed with one of these publishers, they buy your manuscript and you are paid royalties, often accompanied by an advance.

Pros

- Prestige of signing with a well-known publishing house
- Possibility of earning *New York Times* bestseller status

- You receive *some* up-front money.
- You don't have to find a production team to work with; one is assigned to you.
- Wide distribution

Cons

- Limited number of books published each cycle
- Impenetrable gatekeepers
- Lengthy turnaround time from signing to getting to the marketplace
- Before even being considered, you need to have a very large, engaged platform (email list/social following) as one criterion to demonstrate your ability to sell books.
- You need a literary agent to represent you.
- You give up your copyright.
- You lack creative control—in all aspects from messaging to design.
- You don't get to choose your production team.

The one shortsighted mistake I see people make in choosing this option is they chase it solely from a monetary viewpoint. They're fueled by the faulty rationale that they'll get *paid* instead of having to *pay* someone else to help them get published. Being ill-informed about the time and expense that goes into finding a literary agent to represent you, not to mention what it takes to learn how to write effective query letters and book proposals, can create regret and disappointment. Even mastery of all these things doesn't guarantee your book will be picked up by a publisher.

Additionally, people are often disillusioned about the lack of marketing support that comes along with the deal. They don't realize that they will still be responsible for most of the marketing.

On the other hand, if your goal is to achieve a long-held dream of earning the coveted *New York Times* bestseller designation, and you have already built a very large, engaged following, it all might be worth it to you to at least give this path a shot.

With traditional publishing there can be a sense of validation of your work being "good enough." That drives people's decision to seek out this publishing path. One of my past clients, Sharla, fell into this camp.

She had a completed manuscript—a good one. She'd shared it with industry insiders she knew and gotten good feedback on it, but it never got picked up. She got discouraged and tucked her book away where it gathered dust for nearly a decade. She took the rejection as a sign that her work wasn't worthy of being published. When I heard about her experience, I asked her if she'd considered self-publishing. She had a visceral reaction to that. She had a lot of negative beliefs around what that meant, including that it wasn't a legitimate form of publishing.

But she thought about it and did some research, and we talked some more. She came to the realization that self-publishing didn't have to equate with shortcuts that resulted in a sloppy book; it could be done professionally—in a way that was not distinguishable from a book produced by a traditional publisher. And that's what she did. Very successfully, I might add. She's gone on to publish several books since then.

Hybrid Publishing

Hybrid publishing involves author-funded production. Depending on the publisher, you may or may not have to give up your copyright, and there could be a negotiation around future royalties. You have varying degrees of creative control but do have a team to take care of all your production and distribution needs. Marketing of any kind is generally not included, though some hybrid publishing services do offer an add-on or à la carte service you can opt to invest in.

While there are recognized best practices, hybrid publishers vary widely on how well they adhere to those practices. If you choose to go this route, do your research to ensure that their books are professionally produced. Reputable hybrid publishers generally focus on a few specific genres and require you to submit your manuscript for evaluation to ensure it meets their set criteria.

Pros

- You'll have a production team assigned to you.
- It's a faster route to market than traditional publishing.
- You don't have to play the role of project manager.

Cons

- You fund production at a premium.
- You may have limited creative control.
- You don't get to select your production team.
- You generally share royalties with the publisher.

I've heard many great examples of working with a hybrid publisher; I've also heard plenty of nightmarish experiences—poor communication, subpar quality, missed deadlines, and books held "hostage" when removed from active publication.

Most of these situations could have been avoided with research. The problem I generally see here is that people don't know what to look for or what questions to ask—a true case of you don't know what you don't know—so it's worth taking time to educate yourself if it sounds like this could be a good choice for you.

One solid resource is available through the Independent Book Publishing Association. They have established a helpful list of criteria that reputable publishers follow.

Professional Self-Publishing

Yes, I make a point of highlighting "professional" here because I'm not talking about a DIY-style project. (That's possible, but it's not at all the type of book that's going to grow your business, brand, and impact.) I'm referring to a process where you contract with professionals to support you with editing and cover and layout design to meet industry standards. This also involves creating your own publishing imprint—you'll notice that this book, for instance, is published by Magenta Acorn Press; that's my imprint.

Pros

- You have full creative control.
- You set the project timelines.
- You choose your team—at rates without the "middleman" markup.
- You select your publication date.
- You keep 100 percent of the royalties.

- You maintain 100 percent ownership of your intellectual property.

Cons

- The learning curve involved in the process
- You are the project manager (unless you work with a coach who provides this support).
- You are responsible for vetting and contracting your editor and designers.

(Want more information on how to professionally self-publish your book? Check out my Publish Like A Pro guide series by using the QR code in the resources section at the back of this book.)

Professional self-publishing affords a lot of flexibility. You have the option to learn the process yourself or to hire a coach/mentor to support you. You can get referrals from others in your network who've published or find professionals at industry marketplaces like Reedsy.com and the Editorial Freelancers Association.

While it's not the norm, there is something that happens often enough that it's worth mentioning here: Self-published books that perform extremely well can later be picked up by traditional publishers. It's a longer route to proving salability, but it's a way to get your book out more quickly while building an irrefutable case for its commercial value when revisiting the traditional publishing route.

When it comes to the financial side of things and looking at the best choice from the viewpoint of profitability, take a moment to consider these questions to put things in perspective:

1. What is the typical lifetime value of a new client?
2. Based on the investment you're considering, how many new clients would you need to sign to get a tangible return on your investment?

So, what's that look like? Let's say the typical lifetime value of a new client is conservatively $5,000 and the investment you're considering for the professional support needed to create and produce your book is $25,000. In this case you would need the book to help you attract five new clients to pay for itself.

All the added authority, credibility, impact, and future marketing value of the book to generate new clients and opportunities are less tangible—so they're harder to measure. But they can be the biggest sources of return on your investment, so don't leave these factors out in your consideration process.

The bottom line is this: Whatever publishing path you take requires an investment of time and money. The ratio of those things will vary based on the path to publication you choose.

CHAPTER HIGHLIGHTS

- All three paths to publications have pros and cons. The best choice depends on your specific motivations and goals.

- Traditional publishing is the longest, most challenging pathway.

- Hybrid publishing can be a faster path but requires solid research in making your selections.

- Self-publishing, for all its advantages, can also have a steep learning curve.

- There is no professional path to publishing free of investment.

- From a business perspective, forecast your returns as carefully as you scrutinize your investment.

PROFIT WRITE PONDERINGS

1. How quickly do you want and need your book to go to market?

2. Which investments feel best aligned with your business and your goals?

3. Which areas will you dig into further and research before making your publishing decisions?

CHAPTER 15

RALLY TO LAUNCH

We've already talked about why you don't want to quietly release your new book to the world, so let's talk about the alternative: debuting it through a launch.

A launch is a specifically planned and focused time frame in which you create excitement around the fact that your book is officially available for purchase...to create a real buzz around it.

You'll experience the payoff here for keeping your audience looped into your book journey because they are already invested—not just in your book but in seeing you succeed; they've gotten a glimpse into everything you've gone through up to this point, and they're excited to help you spread the word about your new release.

Launches vary widely, influenced by factors like the size of your audience/platform, the topic of your book, your goals around launching, and budgets. For that reason, what I'll share here isn't a comprehensive plan or heavy on tactics but a solid overview of the single most important part of *any* launch: assembling an engaged launch team (sometimes also referred to as a street team).

Think of your launch team like a hype squad. Not only will they purchase your book, but they'll also tell friends, family, and colleagues why they should buy it, too. Oftentimes the visual that pops into my head when thinking about this concept is a clip from that old shampoo commercial from when I was a kid with the line that went something like—"I told two friends about it, and they told two friends, and so on and so on." They allow you to get your book on the radar of people beyond your immediate circle...and in a meaningful way, since you automatically gain a transfer of trust simply by the act of others introducing you and your book to their audience/network.

Having an enthusiastic launch team exponentially grows awareness of and support for your book. Think about your own purchasing behavior. If you're anything like me, there are some people in your circle whose recommendations you trust; they've proved time and again that what they share with you is valuable. I can tell you from personal experience that I purchased many of the books on my bookshelf because they were recommended to me by someone I trusted. In fact, the book that I credit with changing the trajectory of my life—*The Success Principles* by Jack Canfield—was one that was recommended to me; I likely never would have been aware of or purchased it if my son Chris hadn't called me from college one day to tell me I *needed* to read it.

The people who make these kinds of trusted recommendations could even be referred to as microinfluencers, though they wouldn't necessarily categorize themselves that way.

If you've followed the steps laid out throughout this book, people in your social media (and email) circle have gotten to know, like, and trust you even more than they did before you started writing. They know you show up authentically. They've seen snippets of your content. They understand who you are writing this book for and why it's important. They are primed to be ambassadors and champions for your work.

Making the Invitation

By this point you will have shared a teaser letting people know you'll be extending an invitation to join your launch team, but before you make that blanket invitation on social media (we'll talk about that next), reach out personally to invite those who've shown interest or been in your corner.

Throughout your book-writing journey, a certain number of people will consistently show up to cheer you on—engaging in your content and leaving encouraging comments. These are the kinds of people you are focusing on.

As you reach out to invite them to be part of your team, make it personal and heartfelt. And don't forget to let them know what's in it for them. (Behind-the-scenes, first-to-know sneak peeks, learning, prizes, and so on…this will be specific to your launch.) A conversation is always best, but if you're reaching out, say, in a direct message on social media or by text, avoid cutting and pasting the same message and sending it to multiple people. It goes back to our conversation about genuine connection. Make each person feel as special and appreciated as they are.

I want to acknowledge that the thought of this personal reach out sometimes makes people feel a little squirmy inside, brought on by the misguided belief that asking someone to do this *for* you would be putting them out. Or perhaps you've had someone ask you to do something in an off-putting, self-serving way, and you don't want people to think you're like that.

First, the fact that you are concerned about being slimy is the best indicator that you will not show up in that way! You care. You're simply offering an invitation without pressure or expectation. You think enough of them to do so. They may say yes; they may say no. Don't rob them of making that decision by never extending the offer.

More than one author has told me a story about having someone they would have been thrilled to have on their team find out about their launch or about their book release post-launch and being disappointed or hurt that they didn't get asked to participate. People want to help but often just don't know how. They want to be asked, to be included, and to feel special.

If someone comes to your mind, make the ask. You aren't pressuring. You aren't being selfish or self-serving. You are creating an opportunity for them to be involved in something that matters and is meaningful to *them*...which also happens to help get your book—your message—into the hands of the people you labored over this book to help.

What's the worst thing that could happen? Someone may pass on the invitation. No harm, no foul. When you tell someone about that great shoe sale but they don't go buy a pair of shoes, are you devastated? Rejected? Hurt? No. You shared an opportunity, they passed, you continue to be friends. The same is true here. The upside in the case of your launch team is they feel honored that you thought enough about them to personally invite them to be part of your team on such an important project.

The Back End

There are a hundred different ways you can set up your launch team. Maybe you've participated in someone else's and found things you liked and others you didn't. But if you haven't, I highly recommend seizing the opportunity to support fellow authors. In the process you'll get a back-end glimpse of how they are running their launch to get ideas.

(If an Amazon bestselling launch is on your goals list, check out my Launch Your Bestseller series of guides. Check the Resource Roundup page for more details.)

Aside from the nitty-gritty details of specific styles of launches, there is one commonality in all great teams—the ones people really enjoy being part of and participate fully in. It's structured in a way that makes it fast, easy, and fun to help.

FAST by having tasks/tools easily accessible and not burdensome, complicated, or lengthy.

EASY by communicating well, setting out clear timelines, and having everything prepared for them so all they have to do is cut and paste. This includes things like creating graphics and prewritten posts team members can easily share on different social media platforms or in email form.

FUN by incorporating engaging elements in the launch like custom playlists, contests, prizes, Q&A sessions, and other unexpected delights. Not everyone will find all of these elements fun, but if you incorporate a variety, you're going to make everyone feel special and appreciated.

A Word of Caution

I'm guessing the likelihood is greater than good that you've been part of a launch team with a "next-level" type of author—the kind who launch their books with a high level of fanfare...the kind who have already amassed a huge following of engaged followers primed to buy.

When I've supported these types of launches, it's common to see some variation of an offer like this: make a bulk purchase of books (generally 100 books) and receive an invitation to a private mastermind or some other in-person meeting with the author. Typically, that represents a $2,000-ish investment from the followers, which is a fraction of what it would typically cost to meet with the coach/author in person, so it feels like a big ol' win-win-win.

If you have a much smaller audience and/or your fees have not graduated to the level of $10,000–$25,000 offerings, this approach is likely going to go over like a lead balloon with your followers. Add to that, if you are focusing on an Amazon bestseller launch, these kinds of typical presale volumes will not work in your favor since sales are counted at the time they're made rather than all at once on the day of launch. There's a lot of nuance and consideration required here, but suffice it to say, keep *your* ideal audience in mind. What's going to motivate them to buy? What's going to be of mutual benefit? Focus on that, and build a launch strategy that is specific to you and the people you wrote your book for.

CHAPTER HIGHLIGHTS

- Invite enthusiastic, engaged friends, followers, and fans to join your launch team.

- Allow people the opportunity to support you.

- Make the launch process fast, easy, and fun.

- Tailor your launch plan to your audience. The strategy your favorite high-profile author used probably isn't the best choice for you.

PROFIT WRITE PONDERINGS

1. Who do you know who has successfully launched a bestselling book?

2. If you've been part of a book launch team, what did you love and what did you dislike?

3. What will a successful launch look like for you?

4. Who are the people who immediately come to mind as potential launch team members?

CHAPTER 16

KEEP GOING

Sometimes this is hard to hear, but it's important to know that launching your book is *not* where things end. In fact, it's only the beginning.

It's taken a lot of intentional effort to get to this point, and every step that brought you here should be celebrated.

I also think it's important to remind you that it's totally normal to get tired of talking about your book. In fact, at some point it might seem like your book is all you're talking about—like everyone who would want it or cares already knows about it.

Fact check! This is a feeling, *not truth*.

Gloria, a talented client, wrote an acclaimed book on a timeless topic full of value. I reached out to her a few short months after the launch of her book to share a promotional opportunity—

which included a book signing—that I thought was a perfect match for her. She verbalized what many authors feel…

"Wouldn't it be weird to do a book signing so long after the release of my book?"

Excuse me while I remove my filter, but the answer to this question is a big "Hell no!"

The only limitations around timelines are the ones we place on ourselves. If you, like Gloria, write on a subject matter that's timeless rather than trendy, you'll be able to continue promoting it—including book signings—for years to come.

In any circumstance, you *should* have an active promotional plan and be making book-related appearances for a minimum of twelve months.

Post-launch is not the time to take your foot off the gas. Yes, I always advocate for a recovery day or two after launch, but beyond that you'll want to maximize the momentum you've built. It's what will help even more people get to know about you and your book. I'll share a few activities and ways you can do this, but in every single case what is most important is what you do to get mileage out of the "thing."

As we close this book, it bears repeating: The highest level of profit potential for your book is *not* generated by royalties; it is about the opportunities it produces.

Continued marketing and promotion are how you approach this phase. (And as a refresher, that equates to service!) You're the subject matter expert. Find connections to timely topics that keep your book relevant:

- Pitch media and podcasts on relevant angles that lend themselves to at least a mention of your book.
- Host and/or be a guest at book club gatherings featuring your book.
- Continue to create content that relates to your book.
- Nurture community connections that lead to opportunities to join speaker lineups in front of your ideal readers and audience.
- Repurpose content you used during pre-launch to provide a fresh take on topics and create an "omnipresent" effect that has people saying, "I'm seeing you everywhere!"

If you've been on the social media scene for a while, you might remember the early days of Facebook. I became an active user in 2010. With hardly a clue about what I was doing and a tiny real-life network, I started an online community (way before Facebook groups) that quickly grew to over 15,000 people in more than 100 countries...and engagement was through the roof.

Until it wasn't.

We went from an online landscape where everyone who liked your page actually saw your posts to your posts being delivered to only about 10 percent of the community. Today, as the platforms have become more populated and commercialized, the percentage of people who like and follow our page and see our posts is shrinking. Keep in mind that just because you share things related to your book on a frequent basis—even if it feels like you're talking about it ad nauseum—that's not the reality for those following your page. Not everyone you want to see your message sees it at the same time…maybe not even the people you think are seeing it.

I'd be remiss if I didn't tie this back to this simple—and timeless—marketing truth: it generally takes people (the ones who aren't already your raving fans) SEVEN direct exposures to be motivated to act. In the context of this discussion, that means before they pull the trigger on buying your book.

Today two things are incredibly important in thinking about your online network:

1. Share your core message repeatedly.

2. Do it in a way that elicits engagement.

The more people engage with your content, the more the algorithms believe others may want to see your posts, and the more it will be served up to others.

Even in your networks offline, no one is seeing all your emails or announcements or flyers. I think you'll agree that everyone is consumed with their own lives: work, kids, friends, family, school, and so on. It doesn't mean they don't care or aren't supportive. We all have a ton of pulls on our attention. Not to mention the fact that the time people are going to really pay attention is when they're faced with the problem your book solves.

It's your obligation—*every author's obligation*—to keep talking about it...to make it relevant...to help readers find an easy path to you...and to help those who care about the mission of your book—and you—know how and when they can help.

Remember the questions I posed back in chapter 5 when we chatted about choosing the right book idea? This is the reason I asked you to consider if you could still see yourself speaking about this topic in three years. Books won't sell themselves. The moment you decide to stop talking about it is the exact time it becomes irrelevant.

You've done a huge thing in writing your book.

You've distilled years and layers of wisdom and experience.

You've invested time, money, and resources in bringing it to life.

You've written it with the intention of not simply making you money but in creating positive change for your reader.

Don't let all of that fizzle out.

I've provided you with a lot of guidance in these pages, ranging from mindset to getting your book written and launched, but at the end of it all, the most critical point I can leave you with is this:

A profitable book—one that grows your business, brand, and impact—is the one you feel proud to repeatedly share. One you believe in so deeply that you simply cannot keep it to yourself.

With that, my friend, we've reached "The End" as it relates to *this* book.

Now it's time for you to begin.

Go create your book!

ACKNOWLEDGMENTS

> "I can do things you cannot.
> You can do things I cannot.
> Together we can do great things."
>
> MOTHER TERESA

No book is created alone. Some of those who help you cross the finish line are directly involved with its development. Others are people who've provided support, wisdom, and friendship over the course of a lifetime, helping shape the person you are and the work you do. I'm blessed to have both and have deep appreciation for them all. Their encouragement and insights have been invaluable, making this journey both meaningful and rewarding.

I'd like to acknowledge a few remarkable women by name. Each of them has touched my life in unique and meaningful ways—all in some way leading me to write this book: Alexa Bigwarfe, Becky Burroughs, Dr. Brittany Clayborne, Gahmya Drummond-Bey, Sheri Fink, Cami Foerster, Lea Greene, Jen Gottlieb, Beth Jones, Julie Lowe, April Adams Pertuis, and Emma G. Rose.

This book wouldn't be what it is without my talented production team—copy editor Laurel Robinson, proofreader Lucy Morton and designer George Stevens. You've each elevated my work while staying true to my vision, ultimately creating something I'm genuinely proud to have my name on. I'm incredibly grateful to you all.

Last but not least, none of this would be possible without my husband. He supports my audacious ideas and tolerates the erratic schedule it often takes to bring them to fruition. Thank you for always believing in me and being the encourager who reminds me what I'm capable of even on my darkest of days.

RESOURCE ROUNDUP

You can access all the book lists, downloads, courses, and other helpful resources by scanning the QR code below.

Not sure how this works? Follow these simple instructions:

1. Open the camera app on your phone or tablet.
2. Hover device over the QR code until a notification pops up. (No notification? Go to settings and enable QR Code scanning.)
3. Tap the notification and open the link.

CREATE MORE PROFITABILITY

Hey friend!

We've been through a lot on the pages of this book. Now, in the spirit of helping more coaches, entrepreneurs, and business leaders join us in growing their profitability and impact, I come to you with this heartfelt ask:

(Yes…thank you for noticing. I'm walking my talk over here!)

Would you take a moment to leave an honest book review on Amazon for *Profit Write*?

Reviews are incredibly important in the online bookseller space. It wouldn't be an exaggeration to say they're game changing. They can literally make the difference between a book being found, read, and recommended and one that is never seen.

The QR code on this page will take you exactly where you need to go to do this.

Thank you, from the bottom of my very grateful heart.

Lanette

WORK WITH LANETTE

Want to take a deeper dive into creating, publishing, launching, and promoting your book in a way that turns it into a powerful business and impact-making asset?

Lanette works with a limited number of one-on-one clients through coaching, training, and mentorship. She offers this support through online sessions, in-person intensives, and other events.

What You Can Expect

- **Customized Approach:** Receive tailored advice and actionable strategies that align with your vision, goals, and unique objectives.

- **Expert Guidance:** Benefit from Lanette's extensive knowledge and insights in indie publishing.

- **Holistic Support:** From mindset shifts to marketing tactics, get comprehensive support throughout your book creation journey.

- **Exclusive Access:** Work closely with Lanette in an intimate, supportive setting designed to fast-track your success.

Visit www.shegetspublished.com/contact to schedule a Profit Write call with Lanette and discuss the possibilities.

LEARN ABOUT FUTURE EVENTS

Want to stay in the loop about upcoming Profit Write summits, events, and retreats?

Hop on the VIP list at
www.shegetspublished.com/pwevents
for early notification, front-of-the-line offers, and special access.

ABOUT THE AUTHOR

Lanette Pottle is an Amazon international bestselling author and the visionary behind the She Gets Published brand. She has empowered countless entrepreneurs, coaches, and business leaders to transform their expertise into powerful, client-generating books.

As a book coach and publishing mentor, Lanette combines actionable strategies with motivational insights, making the complex process of book creation accessible and enjoyable—even for those who don't yet consider themselves writers.

With a wealth of knowledge in personal and professional development, Lanette approaches every project by drawing on her experience as a certified life coach and business strategist.

When she's not writing or coaching, Lanette enjoys family time and the tranquility of small-town Maine, drawing inspiration from the unbridled joy of her grandchildren and the natural beauty surrounding her.

Stay Connected

- www.instagram.com/shegetspublished
- www.linkedin.com/in/lanettepottle/
- www.shegetspublished.com
- www.shegetspublishedpodcast.com

www.ingramcontent.com/pod-product-compliance
Lightning Source LLC
Chambersburg PA
CBHW060502030426
42337CB00015B/1696